Asset & Liability Management

GARP | Global Association of Risk Professionals

Second edition published in the United States of America by the Global Association of Risk Professionals

111 Town Square Place, 14th Floor
Jersey City, NJ, 07310, USA
Tel: +1 201.719.7210 • Fax: +1 201.222.5022

2nd Floor, Bengal Wing
9A Devonshire Square
London EC2M 4YN, UK
Tel: +44 (0) 20 7397 9630 • Fax: +44 (0) 20 7626 9300
Website: www.garp.org

ISBN: 978-1-933861-07-4

Printed in the United States of America

*This book is dedicated to GARP's Board of Trustees,
without whose support and dedication
to developing the profession of risk management
this book would not have been necessary or possible,
and to the Association's volunteers, representing thousands
of organizations around the globe, who work on
committees and share practical experiences in numerous
global forums and in other ways, and whose goal is
to create a culture of risk awareness.*

Contents

Introduction

The global financial crisis of 2007-2009 has made financial institutions even more aware of their responsibility for managing risks. In the wake of the spectacular, unprecedented, and fundamental transformation of the global financial infrastructure that has followed the crisis, the responsibility of risk managers has changed. At financial institutions worldwide, banks and regulators increasingly rely on the skills, knowledge, and integrity of risk managers to pilot the transforming financial system with improved risk management policies, practices, and systems.

As risk management has moved to the forefront of banking, risk managers are becoming increasingly visible, important, and trusted at banks. This evolution is driven both by banks themselves and by bank supervisors. Banks are increasingly sensitive to the role of risk management in making decisions. Supervisors have come to recognize that better understanding of risk management principles and practices is vital, not only for the success of individual banks, but also for the safety and soundness of the global financial infrastructure.

As a result, bank supervisors have refined regulations that were outlined by the Basel Committee on Banking Supervision in the International Convergence of Capital Measurement and Capital Standards, also known as the Basel II Accord. The changes to Basel II, and new regulations that form the Basel III Accord, reflect the new financial world order, codifying the risk management practices of many highly regarded banks. While this book does not specifically address the Basel II or Basel III Accords, it does reflect the principles and practices—both qualitative and quantitative—that they embrace.

Asset and Liability Management is part of the GARP Financial Risk and Regulation (FRR) series that offers a qualitative introduction to banking risks, risk management, and the international risk-based regulation of banks. The goal of Asset and Liability Management and other related volumes in this series is to ensure that the reader develops a deep understanding of the qualitative aspects of a typical, large bank's risk management activities, including risk assessment, measurement, modeling, and management, across the trading and banking books.

Taken as a whole, the GARP FRR series—Market Risk Management, Credit Risk Management, Operational Risk Management, and Asset and Liability Risk Management—enhances the understanding of specific risks and shows the right questions to ask when qualitatively analyzing the risks of financial instruments or assets. These books create a broad understanding of the key risks banks face and how these risks can be best managed.

Understanding the specific sources of risks is essential in the management process of measuring, monitoring, and managing risk. The material is presented in a user-friendly format enabling readers to understand the key qualitative risk factors and how they drive bank risk management. Each book contains numerous examples of actual financial events, as well as case studies, diagrams, and tables that explain these complex relationships. Overall, these volumes foster a better understanding of why and how financial risks emerge and how these risks can impact individual financial assets, financial institutions, financial systems, and ultimately, the global financial infrastructure.

Students who successfully complete market, credit, operational, and asset and liability risk management readings will gain a broad understanding of how the various risks reinforce each other. Such students are strongly encouraged to sit for GARP's International Certificate in Financial Risk and Regulation, an integrated look at the chief risks financial institutions face and how to best manage them. To complete the program, students may decide to take a certification exam.

These readings contain several technical terms used in banking and risk management. While the material requires a fundamental understanding of finance and banking, the intended readers are not practicing risk managers but bankers who want to have a better understanding of the qualitative factors affecting risks and who have familiarity with fundamental banking and finance concepts. This study text has adopted the standard codes used by banks throughout the world to identify currencies for the purposes of trading, settlement, and the displaying of market prices. The codes, set by the International Organization for Standardization (ISO), avoid the confusion that could result from many currencies having similar names. For example, the text uses USD for the US dollar, GBP for the British pound, EUR for the euro, and JPY for the Japanese yen.

Acknowledgements

Asset and Liability Management, (previously entitled Integrated Risk Management), a volume in the GARP Financial Risk and Regulation series, has been developed, and now revised, under the auspices of the Banking Risk and Regulation Committee at GARP who guided and reviewed the work of the contributing authors.

The Committee would like to thank David C. Shimko, Ph.D., Peter Went, Ph.D., Amanda Neff, Graeme Skelly, Christian Thornæs, Andrew Cunningham and other members of GARP for their contributions to this latest edition.

Introduction to Asset and Liability Management

Asset and Liability Management, a volume in the GARP FRR series, focuses on asset and liability management by analyzing how risk drives capital management decisions for banks. It consists of four chapters: the first focuses on the role and responsibilities of the ALCO committee and Treasury, the second focuses on the interest rate and equity risk in the banking book, the third focuses on liquidity risk, and the fourth focuses on capital management.

In analyzing the role and function of Treasury and the ALCO, the readings focus on the role of Treasury under several bank models, as well as the policy foundation and the specific limit structure that guide activities. In analyzing the interest rate and equity risk in the banking book, the readings focus on the role a bank's treasury function plays in managing the comprehensive risk exposures of the bank, including the measurement and management of asset and liability exposures, and various alternative approaches to better understand these. In analyzing the liquidity risk, the readings focus on the various types of liquidity, sources of liquidity problems, and the potential costs of mismanaging liquidity risk. In analyzing capital management in banks, the readings focus on the types and roles of capital, and how risk adjusted capital has evolved as an important tool to manage banks.

CHAPTER 1

ALCO and the Organization of ALM

We begin with an overview of asset and liability management (ALM), ALM processes, and the role of Treasury. Interest rate risk in the banking book is covered in Chapter 2 and liquidity risk management is covered in Chapter 3. Bank capital management is also sometimes considered part of treasury risk, but it can also fall in the strategic planning area. This topic is discussed in detail in Chapter 4.

On completion of this chapter the reader will have an improved understanding of:

- The role of the treasury function in different types of banks
- Types of treasury risk
- The importance of asset and liability management (ALM) in banks
- The objectives of an ALM program

1.1 The Role of the Treasury

The Treasury function plays a significant role in managing a bank's assets and liabilities, its liquidity, and its capital. The Treasury can also play many different roles in a bank. The exact roles vary significantly depending on the business model adopted by the bank.

Most treasury functions take an active role in managing the bank's balance sheet capital: the debt and equity the bank has raised to finance its assets. As capital can either be equity capital or debt, it thus has multiple meanings. For instance, accounting equity capital is the equity capital the bank has raised from shareholders and from its earnings. Typically, equity capital satisfies regulatory capital, but there may be types of capital other than equity capital that are eligible to meet regulatory capital requirements. Additionally, the financing sources may also include debt: both long-term borrowings and deposits.

Some forms of capital require no interest payments (such as equity and reserves), but most capital comes in the form of interest-bearing deposits, interbank loans, and securities. The collective capital is invested to generate a cash return, the risk of that return depends on how the capital is allocated to different types of interest-bearing assets. This gives the bank an interest "net position" (it earns interest on the assets and pays interest on the funding) that must be managed to avoid volatile profit and losses as interest rates move. This is one type of interest rate risk the bank bears. Fluctuations in interest rates also create "equity risk" for the bank as the value of its assets and liabilities change.

While the bank treasury performs standard corporate treasury functions, such as security issuance, cash forecasting and management, financial decisions, and insurance, the role of the treasury in a bank goes beyond these standard areas due to the large number of financial functions in the bank. Every bank has slightly different functions, but a large number fit into one of two models: a commercial/retail model, or a commercial/retail with investment banking model. The typical function of the treasury in these two bank types is described below.

1.1.1 A Commercial/Retail Only Bank Model

A typical commercial/retail bank model focuses its asset strategy on commercial and retail loans, and funds the loans using a combination of equity, retained earnings, deposits, publicly issued bonds and interbank loans. It may seem that a bank of this type would focus on its underwriting risk and, as long as there were not too many commercial or retail defaults, the bank would perform well. However, this simplification is incorrect. It is possible that the bank could have an extremely good underwriting department but could still lose a great deal of money due to fluctuations in interest rates. Interest rates could affect its income adversely and could also affect its balance sheet adversely.

As an example of how interest rates could have this effect, suppose the bank had entered into a number of long-term commercial and retail loans at the fixed rates that were prevailing at the time the loans were originated. If interest rates subsequently rose, the bank would have to pay higher interest rates to its depositors and would have to pay higher rates on its debt to the extent the debt interest rate was linked to floating indices, or to the extent the debt used to fund the loans was of a shorter maturity than the loans. However, the interest it was receiving on its fixed rate loans would be unchanged. As a result, if rates rose, the bank could actually end up in a negative cash flow position even in the absence of defaults.

As an example of balance sheet effects, if rates rose, the same bank would see its fixed rate assets drop in value, although that effect would be offset by a reduction in the value of its fixed rate liabilities. Floating rate assets and liabilities would not change much in value. This affects the value of the equity of the bank, since equity is the difference between assets and liabilities. For that reason, this risk is sometimes called equity risk. If fixed rate assets were much greater than fixed rate liabilities, as would be the case for most commercial/retail banks, rising interest rates would damage the bank's equity value.

Treasury departments in commercial/retail banks are likely to manage the net interest rate risk in their banking book directly with market counterparties by operating a derivatives trading desk. In the bank described above, to protect against rising interest rates, the bank would enter into interest rate swaps where it paid fixed rates and received floating rates to offset the risk of its fixed rate assets (see Chapter 3 in the Market Risk Management book). The objective, as explained later in this section, is to manage the interest margin of the bank: the return the bank earns on its assets such as loans and investments, and the funding cost of these, such as the interest paid on deposits.

International commercial/retail banks have foreign exchange risk in their operations due to foreign operating expenses such as salaries and property leases. In these cases, the management of the attendant foreign exchange exposure will often fall to the treasury as well.

Some banks treat their treasury unit as a cost center that primarily focuses on managing interest rate and foreign exchange risk. Others run their treasury function as a profit-making business unit. This is particularly true in developed markets, while in emerging and developing markets the Treasury supports the overall activities of the bank. Larger banks in the emerging and developing markets may task their treasury function with managing their foreign currency exposure.

For instance, if a bank has substantial commercial and retail business, and the currency in which it primarily operates is not a major currency, then the Treasury may manage the interest rate risk positions for profit. The constant business coming from the lending and deposit gathering of the bank's commercial and retail business results in it being well positioned to exploit its commercial position in domestic currency interest rate risk markets. When the same commercial position results in the bank executing significant orders from its customers for foreign currency transactions, the Treasury may in fact run complex trading operations.

Banks may operate in a heavily traded currency where there are substantial institutional counterparties, including investment banks and hedge funds. In this situation it is likely that a commercial and retail bank's treasury operations will primarily be focused on ensuring that the risks generated by the bank's businesses are covered in the market. Such treasury operations are commonly known as cover operations. They make sure that the profits generated by the customer business are not damaged by the failure to manage the inherent market risk, e.g., the interest rate or foreign exchange risk in the banking book.

1.1.2 A Commercial/Retail Bank with an Investment Banking Operation Business Model

For banks with an investment banking operation actively engaged in trading market risk and managing it for profit, the treasury function is likely to be primarily concerned with the effective transfer of interest rate risk in the banking book to the investment bank at a fair transfer price. Here a central treasury function serves other parts of the bank and provides a support function to those commercial and investment banking operations that are more directly client focused.

The central Treasury may be responsible for managing the retail market risk function of a commercial/retail bank with an investment banking operation. However, some banks with investment banking operations permit their commercial and retail businesses to manage their individual banking book risks directly with the investment banking operation. In this business model the Treasury takes on the role of monitoring and regulating the management of interest rate risk in the banking book, while retaining its group-wide liquidity and capital management activities.

Ensuring the smooth flow of such business will require "running"/taking on trading positions to manage these risks. However, such risks are likely to be of a limited nature.

In general terms, this is the model followed by JPMorgan Chase, as described in their 2013 Annual Report. Most other banks that do not have the same size and strategic breadth as JPMorgan Chase tend to follow the first approach: the commercial/retail banking approach.

1.2 Treasury Risk

Treasury risk is defined as the risk of loss in the activities of a bank's Treasury. It is also sometimes used to mean ALM risk alone. Since every Treasury operates slightly differently, however, the term "Treasury risk" can be ambiguous. Here is one example of an integrated bank treasury function:

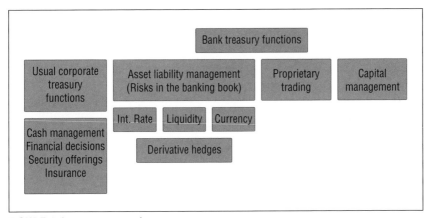

FIGURE 1.1 Treasury Risk

To avoid confusion in the rest of this volume, we will refer to specific treasury functions where applicable and avoid the generalized term "Treasury risk."

1.2.1 Selecting Techniques to Measure Interest Rate and FX Risk

Interest rate risk, like most types of market risk, can be expressed either in the spot or in the forward dimension.

Spot interest rate risk starts immediately and lasts for a specific period, while forward interest rate risk starts at a point in the future and lasts for a specific period after that.

The risk is directional, as in "up" versus "down," and either movement can be costly depending on whether investors are long with respect to short-term fixed income instruments, or short with respect to long-term floating rate instruments.

For further reference to interest rate risk, see Chapter 1.6.2: Interest Rate Risk in the *Market Risk Management* book in this Financial Risk and Regulation (FRR) series.

Foreign exchange (FX) transactions are typically settled once, so foreign exchange risk is a forward type of risk. FX risk is directional too, exposing long and short positions in a currency to weakening and strengthening of that currency respectively.

The forward foreign exchange rate is constructed from three factors (spot FX rate, interest rate in base currency, and interest rate in quoted currency), while forward interest rates are constructed from two factors (short- and long-term interest rates on the same yield curve).

For further reference to foreign exchange risk, see Chapter 1.6.1: Foreign Exchange Risk in the *Market Risk Management* book in this Financial Risk and Regulation (FRR) series.

Interest Rate Risk Measures
It can be difficult to "see" the value of a change in an interest rate. It is therefore helpful to imagine being either long or short fixed income or floating rate instruments. This makes it easier to translate a change in interest rates to an equivalent change in price, or value. "Present Value of a Basis Point" (PVBP, PV01, DV01, or duration) is an excellent tool to convert a 1 bp (basis point = 0.01%) change in yield into an equivalent measure in price.

Despite the importance of PV01 as a method of describing interest rate risk, it suffers from a specific weakness: PV01 is not very good at describing value change due to large changes in interest rates. To capture this element of risk, a bond analyst typically looks at the convex relationship between bond prices and bond yields. The longer the maturity or the lower the coupon the more convex the relationship. And the more convexity, the greater the risk.

However, bank treasurers do not have the bond analysts' luxury of looking at a single duration at a time. They must simultaneously manage multiple durations right across the yield curve and that yield curve rarely moves up or down in strictly parallel fashion. A pragmatic approach to managing ALM risk and the maturity transformation process is therefore to divide the future up into a number of time slots, or buckets, and then risk manage each as if all cash flows in each bucket were identical. This enables the Treasurer to look at each bucket as if it was a single large cash flow expiring on a single day and it makes the risk management process much less complicated.

This practicality explains the use and popularity of PV01 in ALM: one PV01 per time bucket. But why is convexity used so sparingly, if at all, in the heat of the moment by a Treasury responsible for a trillion dollar balance sheet? In reality:

1. Most banks try to match-fund long-term assets, or at least hedge the funding cost with interest rate swaps, and, by doing so, make them much less susceptible, or even immune, to convexity risk.
2. Most banks try to profit from interest rate discrepancies between different maturities in the very short end of the yield curve (i.e., less than one year). There is very little convexity in durations of less than one year.

This explains the lower propensity for some banks to actively use convexity as a risk management tool.

However, larger banks with bigger IT budgets have made a further leap in the process of interest rate risk management. Instead of using proxies (duration, convexity) to describe the risk in their books, they use "heavy iron" computing power to conduct full repricing (Monte Carlo Simulation[1]-based, if necessary) of their positions at all relevant yield curve points. This development is several orders of magnitude more complicated and expensive to build and use, but the increased precision is worth the effort, if the bank is able to afford the cost.

Foreign Exchange Risk Measures
Most banks have at least a proportion of their assets and liabilities denominated in currencies other than their financial reporting currency. This gives rise to foreign exchange risk.

Using a variety of hedging tools (cross-currency interest rate swaps, cross-currency basis swaps, FX swaps, FX options) it is possible to immunize the FX risk component in the balance sheet of a bank. Deciding whether to use these tools, or not to use them, is part of executing the ALM policy.

EXAMPLE

The 1990s and early 2000s were characterized by extraordinarily low JPY interest rates prompting the spread of the "Yen Carry Trade." Banks borrowed in JPY to fund assets in other currencies, at the expense of taking a foreign currency (JPY) revaluation risk. Being a

---

1   A problem-solving technique used to approximate the probability of certain outcomes by running multiple trial runs, called simulations, using random variables. investopedia.com

major exporting economy, the Bank of Japan kept interest rates low to ensure exports were not hurt by an appreciating yen. This policy effectively took away most of the devaluation risk, fueling the carry trade even more.

Foreign exchange exposure can be quantified in pips (normally the fourth decimal point in the quote) or in interest rate differential terms. The pip measure is useful in a trading context, while the interest rate differential measure is more meaningful in an ALM context.

For example, assume a three-month GBP LIBOR-based asset yields 3% and that this asset could be funded by a three-month GBP LIBOR-based liability at 2% for an effective profit of 1% to the bank. If at the same time the bank can fund in three-month JPY LIBOR at 1%, the profit would increase to 2%, but at the risk of the JPY strengthening. If a cross-currency basis swap GBP-JPY is quoted at 60 bp for equivalent three-month/three-month periods, it would be possible for the bank to neutralize JPY FX risk and lock in a profit of 3% – 1% – 0.6% = 1.4%: that is, 0.4% better than funding in GBP, yet with a full GBP-JPY FX risk hedge.

1.2.2 Internal controls, procedures, and reporting requirements

A modern treasury operation must have appropriate internal controls, procedures, and reporting requirements that are in line with industry best practices and reflect requirements elsewhere in the bank.

The following is a sample list of some of the most important areas in which to implement controls:

Category	Type of Control	Example
Risk management framework and governance	The board is ulitimately responsible for the execution of, and compliance with, the risk policies and internal controls. This may be delegated to an audit or risk committee.	The board receives reports on treasury activities, including compliance with policy. People with specialist skills may be required to sit on this committee.
Policy and procedures	The policy should include a table of specific delegations. For example, who can approve new financial facilities, negotiate facilities, draw down loan facilities, etc.	Delegations should be stated in the treasury policy document as well as position descriptions. These delegations may also be built into treasury and payment systems (e.g. approval limits).
Organizational structure	Treasury is subject to regular review by internal audit, external audit, or by peer auditors.	Treasury function included in internal audit plan
Limits	To be stated in treasury policy: • Counterparty limits are ultimately approved by the board • Credit limits • Settlement limits • Investment limits	Limits should be reviewed annually and approved by the board. To the extent possible, limits are loaded in the treasury system. This will depend on the sophistication of the treasury systems. Credit limits are usually based on information from an external rating agency.
Personnel: training, compliance, and performance	Settlement and support staff have appropriate education.	Self-explanatory.
Reporting	Daily settlement reports Cash-flow reports Bank account balances from all sources Exposure reports Limit reports	Daily settlement report for dealers and settlement staff Cash flow forecasts from business units Bank account and transaction listings from the electronic banking system Maturity diaries for dealers Counterparty limit reports for dealers and compliance staff Transaction audit trail reports End of day reports from clearing houses for matching to bank account information. Reports are provided to business units of their net currency position

Operational reports	Exception reports.	Exception reports are provided to senior management and the board, especially relating to policy breaches.
Risk management activities	Dealers must check position/ exposure limits and credit limits prior to dealing.	Process to check limits including counterparty limits and exposure limits in treasury systems.
Post-deal controls	There should be no undue concentration of dealing with a particular counterparty.	Limits are set for each counterparty in treasury policy statement.
Operations (settlements)	Payments are initiated by one operator, confirmed and released by another separate party.	All payments require at least two staff to execute.
Controls over settlement	No deals are to be settled by any dealer in the company.	Self-explanatory.
Reconciliation of bank accounts and treasury records to the general ledger	Estimated end of day balances are compared with actual next day, with investigation of significant variations from anticipated balances.	Compare the bank balance in the treasury system with the one shown in the bank statement.
Cash management	Authorized bank signatories are kept up to date in the register. This register is to be reviewed annually.	Self-explanatory.
Physical security (records/ key systems)	Important legal documents such as ISDA (International Swap and Derivative Dealers Association) agreements are stored securely.	Stored in a safe, or scanned and stored electronically.
Monitoring of risk management activities	All new financial investment products must be examined for risks and approved by the board.	Self-explanatory.
Treasury infrastructure	Obtain independent valuations of any models and spreadsheets used.	All treasury software and systems have been subject to rigorous internal and external testing.

FIGURE 1.2 Sample Controls

The checklist above[2] outlines the controls typically found in well-controlled environments where there is a treasury or treasury type activity.

---

2   See: www.cpaaustralia.com.au/~/media/corporate/allfiles/document/professional-resources/business/internal-controls-for-treasury.pdf

1.3 Asset and Liability Management Committee (ALCO) Activities

While the treasury usually manages day-to-day ALM risk, it often does so under the oversight of an Asset Liability Committee (ALCO) or in some cases the Risk Management Committee. The role of the traditional ALCO is defined by *The American Banker:*[3]

A committee, usually comprising senior managers, responsible for managing assets and liabilities to maximize income and safety over the long run. In a financial institution, the ALCO is usually responsible for asset and liability distribution, asset and liability pricing, balance sheet size, funding, spread management, and interest rate sensitivity management.

In most banks, asset and liability management has the primary objective of managing the impact of interest rate risk in the bank's balance sheet and ensuring that the interest rate risk inherent in the bank's underlying business does not disrupt the production of a stable income stream over time.

Asset and liability management is not just concerned with managing risk and stabilizing business value. It is also concerned with:

■ Maintaining the desired liquidity structure of a bank, as seen in the next chapter
■ Other factors affecting the structure and composition of a bank's balance sheet
■ Circumstances impacting the stability of income the bank generates over time

Numerous problems arise from the need to balance the structure and composition of a bank's balance sheet. Many of these are related to the problems international banks face because their capital structures are dominated by their home currency, but their earnings and many of their assets and liabilities are in other currencies. This introduces foreign exchange risk into the bank's earnings (see Chapter 2 in the *Market Risk Management* book in this series). For example, the present and future profits from overseas operations may be volatile when translated into the bank's domestic currency due to changes in the exchange rate, which are affected by differences in interest rates. Similarly, domestic currency denominated capital that has been allocated to overseas operations supports an asset structure denominated in a different, foreign, currency. Since exchange rates and profitability can change, the dual effect of these changes introduce

---

3   See www.americanbanker.com/glossary.html

volatility into the capital requirements and may reduce the ability to meet regulatory minimum standards.

Asset and liability management is often described as using risk management techniques employed by bond portfolio managers and applying them to the repricing of interest rates on retail assets and liabilities (see Chapter 3 in the *Market Risk Management* book in this series). The reason for this is that the cash flows, investments, and loans the bank holds on its balance sheet, and deposits with which it finances these assets can be modeled as if they were cash flows generated by bonds. While in many ways this is true, the asset and liability manager has to recognize the following:

- A bank's balance sheet is a dynamic collection of assets and liabilities because new loans and deposits are continuously being made/received while others mature.
- Repricing of the assets and liabilities on a bank's balance sheet is not all contractual since there are often significant timing differences between changes in market rates affecting the pricing of wholesale credit and deposit products and changes in the interest rates on retail credit and deposit products.
- There is frequently little or no correlation between retail product and wholesale product rates for pricing assets and liabilities. This is because many retail products are driven by marketing considerations, and these impose restrictions (that do not apply to wholesale products) on the repricing of retail products.
- Retail products frequently include embedded options which are often not rationally exercised, such as the right to prepay certain retail credit products without significant penalties. In contrast, wholesale products typically carry penalties for repayment or include rights to terminate wholesale contracts on very different terms than are common in retail products.

There are several reasons why a bank with a significant number of retail customers may find its balance sheet shape and structure difficult to manage. They include:

- Banks with a wide retail base are often driven by relationship considerations and not simply contractual obligations, i.e., they are customer focused.
- Attracting and retaining customers often involves offering retail products whose features are different from wholesale market products,

and because of inherent differences in the structure of the different types of products, managing the risk of retail products using tools designed for managing the risk of wholesale products may be difficult.

■ Pricing of retail products often has more to do with marketing considerations rather than prevailing market price, which drives the pricing of wholesale products.

■ The way retail customers behave in relation to the retail banking products they hold often results in the apparent contractual obligations of the parties, providing a poor description of the actual nature of the obligations. For example it may be contractually possible to withdraw funds from a savings account on 30 days' notice, but the customer has a right to leave the money on account indefinitely. The balance on such accounts may behave more like a three-year deposit account than either a 30-day deposit account or a perpetual account.

It is often these inter-related customer and product behavior features that give rise to the need to monitor and manage the stability of net interest income (or present value of the business) and the liquidity of these balances.

EXAMPLE

P-Bank plans to launch a campaign to increase local deposits with a six-month "teaser" rate. If the campaign is successful, new deposits will be added to the bank's liability structure, but the risk of those deposits will be uncertain. For example, will the deposits be withdrawn once the teaser rate is no longer in effect? Also, will the new depositors have the same average characteristics as the current depositors? Some may hold their deposits longer, due to the in-convenience and cost of changing banks. Others may withdraw the deposits sooner than six months, being more sensitive to other banks' competing offers. Or perhaps the new depositor base will have completely different liquidity needs, compared to the current depositor base.

Because of the uncertainty of depositor retention, P-Bank's current and future exposure to interest rates is unknown and variable.

1.3.1 Currency and Interest Rate Risk

There are four common ways of analyzing interest rate risk in an ALM context:

■ Repricing risk analysis for measuring yield curve risk, including
  ● Repricing schedule
  ● Rate sensitivity gap
  ● Repricing gap analysis

- Static simulation
- Dynamic simulation for measuring optionality
■ Analyzing basis risks for measuring the effect on interest income
  Report of basis risks within each time band/bucket
■ Fund transfer pricing (FTP) for measuring the effect on interest income
  - FTP report detailing profit contribution from Asset, Funding, and Liability spread respectively (see Figure 1.3 below)
■ Duration
  - Duration gap model

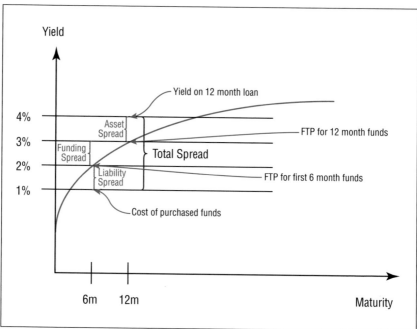

FIGURE 1.3   FTP Analysis of Asset, Funding, and Liability Spreads

1.3.2 ALM and Liquidity Risk

Liquidity management is a key component in managing bank balance sheets. It ensures the bank maintains sufficient cash and liquid assets to meet expected deposit withdrawal and disbursement demands, and to pay expenses.

Asset and Liability Management is another key component and is defined as the process of planning, organizing, and controlling asset and liability volumes, maturities, rates, and yields, so interest rate risk can be minimized and profits remain acceptable.

The two components are effectively intertwined. Without adequate management of this co-dependency, it would be difficult to imagine low-cost funds being consistently available to meet expected deposit withdrawals.

1.3.3 Investment Strategies and Funding Guidelines

For classic commercial banks, an investment strategy is mostly about deciding on the asset mix: which assets should the bank hold and what should the relative weight between them be. Typical assets are:

1. Cash
2. Consumer loans
3. Commercial/SME loans
4. Corporate loans

Each asset type comes with a specific profit/loss profile and an interest rate risk profile.

Once the asset mix has been agreed, the bank needs to decide how the assets should be funded. Typical funding alternatives are:

1. Consumer deposits
2. Corporate deposits
3. Financial institution deposits
4. Securitization issues
5. Long-term bond issues in the bank's own name
6. Repurchase agreements

With the asset and liability strategies in hand, a bank's management needs policy guidelines for cash flow and duration gaps in order to maximize the profit potential, while minimizing the risk in the balance sheet.

1.3.4 Production of Mismatch and Gap Reports

The following reports are used traditionally for ALM Gap Analysis:

- Cash flow reports, focusing on asset and liability maturities and mismatches
- Liquidity reports, focusing on asset liquidity, a weak form of the Liquidity Coverage Ratio (LCR), an international standard for short-term liquidity
- Rate sensitivity reports, focusing on both net and cumulative rate exposure mismatches/gaps
- Volatility reports for assets/liability items with embedded optionality (callable bonds, MBS, etc.)
- Value-at-risk (VaR) reports, to identify how evenly the bank's ALM risk is spread over the maturity spectrum

Each of the above reports is divided into time bands/buckets in order to clearly identify net exposures that can be rate sensitive and/or require refunding. All reports are subject to regular stress testing to identify weaknesses, if any.

Historically, these reports were produced for internal consumption only, with only key numbers passed on to regulators. However, in the aftermath of the global financial crisis of 2007-2009 both the Basel III Accords and national regulators are requiring banks to disclose not only their ALM strategy, but also the reports with which it is managed and explanations for deviations from agreed plans.

A contemporary wording (January 2013) for these reports is to be found in the BCBS Basel III Liquidity Coverage Ratio document, Monitoring Tools, Paragraph 176, (http://www.bis.org/publ/bcbs238.pdf):

1. *Contractual maturity mismatch:*
   a. Contractual cash and security inflows and outflows from all on- and off-balance sheet items, mapped to defined time bands based on their respective maturities.

2. *Concentration of funding*
   a. Funding liabilities sourced from each significant counterparty as a percentage of total liabilities
   b. Funding liabilities sourced from each significant product/instrument as a percentage of total liabilities
   c. List of asset and liability amounts by significant currency

3. *Available unencumbered assets*
   a. Available unencumbered assets that are marketable as collateral in secondary markets, and
   b. Available unencumbered assets that are eligible for central banks' standing facilities

4. *LCR by significant currency*
   a. To calculate: Foreign Currency LCR = Stock of HQLA in each significant currency / Total net cash outflows over a 30-day time period in each significant currency. HQLA are High Quality Liquid Assets (see Glossary)
   Note: The numbers are calculated net of FX hedges.

5. *Market-related monitoring tools*
   Supervisors must monitor data at the following levels to focus on potential liquidity difficulties:
   a. Market-wide information (equity, debt, FX, rates, commodities market data)
   b. Information on the financial sector (track whether the financial sector mirrors economy as a whole)
   c. Bank-specific information (track market perception of risk at individual bank organization)

1.4 Board Policies for ALM and ALCO

Advisory wording and regulatory requirements for Boards of Directors include the following themes (quoted from the US Federal Housing Finance Administration (FHFA)[4] as an example of the US Interagency Agreement on Interest Rate Risk Management). These rules apply to all US financial institutions.

Board and senior management oversight is the cornerstone of an effective risk management process. The board and senior management have the responsibility to understand the nature and magnitude of interest rate risk being taken.

Successful risk management requires an informed board, capable management, and appropriate staffing.

For its part, a board of directors must:

---

4   See: Interagency Advisory on Interest Rate Risk, FHFA version, Sept. 2013,
http://www.fhfa.gov/SupervisionRegulation/Documents/Interest_Rate_Risk_Management_
Module_Final_Version_1.0_508.pdf

1. Establish clear strategic direction and interest rate risk tolerance limits and identify the senior managers who have the authority and responsibility for managing this risk.
2. Maintain comprehensive and up-to-date policies and procedures. Policies should be reviewed and approved at least annually.
3. Monitor performance and overall interest rate risk profile, ensuring a prudent amount of interest rate risk is maintained, is supported by adequate capital, and complies with regulatory requirements and internal policy parameters.
4. Confirm the adherence to sound risk management principles that facilitate the identification, measurement, monitoring, and control of interest rate risk.
5. Provide adequate resources devoted to interest rate risk management. Effective risk management requires both technical and human resources.
6. Ensure sufficient independence of the risk management, monitoring, and control functions from the position-taking functions.
7. Have directors with practical interest rate risk skills and experience due to the complexity of managing interest rate risk. Further, the board should receive ongoing training on interest rate risk in order to ensure the directors understand the regulated entity's interest rate risk exposure.
8. Establish a system for ensuring corrective action is taken to address regulatory, internal/external audit, and consultant findings.

Senior management is responsible for managing interest rate risk. In that capacity, senior management should:

1. Develop and implement procedures and practices that translate the board's goals, objectives, and risk tolerances into operating standards that are well understood by personnel.
2. Ensure adherence to the lines of authority and responsibility that the board has established for measuring, managing, and reporting interest rate risk exposures.
3. Oversee the implementation and maintenance of management information and other systems that identify, measure, monitor, and control interest rate risk.
4. Establish effective interest rate internal controls.
5. Establish effective interest rate risk internal controls.

1.4.1 Overall Balance Sheet Structure

The overall balance sheet structure of a bank depends on a multitude of factors, not least of which is the business model it has adopted. Among the areas that influence its balance sheet structure and must therefore be reviewed regularly to conform to regulations are:

- Setting the cost of capital
- Capital stress testing
- Capital planning
- Return on (risk-adjusted) capital calculations
- Capital allocation within the organization
- Economic capital calculation
- Capital adequacy reporting
- Regulatory Risk Weighted Assets calculation

Strategically, the balance sheet must be structured to make it resilient, which would normally require high levels of capital and long-term funding, but could also include an emphasis on short-term assets. Another thing to consider is the asset turnover ratio, expected to be high in an investment bank or trading organization and correspondingly low in a relationship banking context. Trading operations have higher asset turnover velocity than do lending banks, allowing them to be more thinly capitalized—relatively speaking—than banks with semi-liquid or illiquid positions in the banking book.

The following Figures describe a reasonable balance sheet base case, as well as deteriorated scenarios with changes in either assets or liabilities.

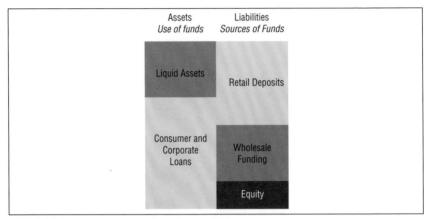

FIGURE 1.4   Base Case Bank Balance Sheet

Banks with a ratio of risky assets to equity that is higher than 1 (see Figure 5) are subject to severe solvency problems in case of deterioration of the quality of the risky assets.

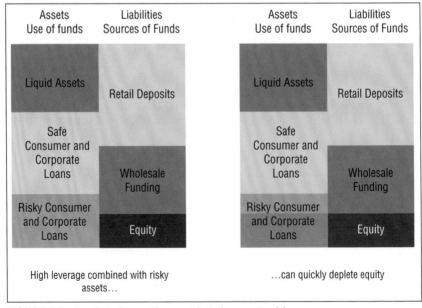

FIGURE 1.5   Bank Balance Sheet with Solvency Problems

Banks with a "flight deposits"-to-liquid assets ratio higher than 1 are subject to severe liquidity problems in case of deterioration in the volume of "flight deposits." ("Flight deposits" are those that are likely to be withdrawn as soon as there is any sign of trouble at the bank.)

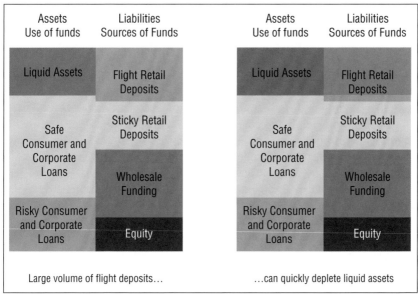

Large volume of flight deposits…   …can quickly deplete liquid assets

FIGURE 1.6 Bank Balance Sheet with Liquidity Problems

1.4.2 Asset and Liability Mix for Retail and Wholesale Operations

Retail banking assets are, with exceptions, typically floating rate for the credit card business and fixed rate for other lending, including consumer and auto loans. In the US, mortgages are typically fixed rate, although in the UK and many other countries they are typically floating rate.

Commercial and corporate banking assets are mostly floating rate. However, while floating rate benchmarks in consumer and commercial lending are set by the bank, corporate loan customers are often given a choice between a number of benchmarks (i.e., one-month, three-month, or six-month LIBOR, Prime/Base rate, Commercial Paper rate).

Given the variety of possible interest rate profiles for bank assets, the ALM policy must set out appropriate targets and benchmarks that must be followed by the bank's asset gathering divisions.

In parallel, the ALM policy must set out realistic objectives for the bank's funding. It should detail permitted maximum interest rate gaps between lending and funding, suggested diversification of the sourcing of funds, and permitted funding instruments, among other things.

The general rule for prudent Treasury management specifies that asset and liability maturities/durations should be as closely matched as possible.

1.4.3 Guidelines for Pricing, Term, and Maturity for Permitted Activities

The ALM policy should set out guidelines for pricing, term, and maturity of permitted lending, money market, interest rate derivatives, and foreign exchange funding and trading activities.

Retail, commercial, and corporate bank assets are priced differently, in accordance with the features of their respective markets, but are all subject to ALCO policy levels of minimum return in order to discourage indiscriminate asset build-ups in the balance sheet.

Consumer, and to some extent commercial, credit margins are among the highest in a bank, while deposit rates are among the lowest. The resulting Net Interest Income (NII) for this part of the bank's business creates room to allow for temporary competitive pricing to attract new customers and it also provides a cushion against expected credit losses.

The NII margin in the corporate and institutional business and bid-ask spreads in traded markets are subject to significant competitive pressure and are much lower as a result. This does not give the bank much room for temporary competitive pricing to gain new customers and the NII in the corporate banking business is often barely large enough to cover expected losses.

ALM policy guidelines for term and maturity must be sufficiently granular to allow the bank's lending and funding activities to continue, while limiting the proportions of long term assets and short term liabilities.

1.5 Asset and Liability Management (ALM) Risk

The income stream of many banks is dominated by their NII, the difference between the interest charged on loans (and other assets) and the interest cost of raising deposits (and other liabilities). The current value (net present value) of the stream of NII over time is the major contributor to the value of the bank.

EXAMPLE

Bank M has USD 100 million in deposits it pays 2% interest on, and USD 20 million in equity it pays no interest on. The loan portfolio of USD 120 million earns an average rate of 6%. If rates stay the same, the NII will be $[120 \times (0.06)] - [100 \times (0.02)] = $ USD 5.2 million per year. If the bank is able to earn this in perpetuity, the present value would be 5.2/0.05 = USD 104 million at a discount rate of 5%. The present value of NII is an asset of the bank on its economic balance sheet, and the value of the equity balances assets and liabilities.

Before Rate Increase				After Rate Increase			
Assets		**Liabilities**		**Assets**		**Liabilities**	
Loans	120	Deposits	100	Loans	120	Deposits	100
PV NII	104	Equity	124	PV NII	84	Equity	104
Economic value of Assets	224	Economic value of Financing	224	Economic value of Assets	204	Economic value of Financing	204

FIGURE 1.7: Economic Value of the Bank

This table outlining the economic value of the bank is a "balance sheet" that does not record the assets and liabilities of the bank in accounting terms, but rather in economic value terms. Economic value reflects the earnings potential including the market value of the assets. The interest rate change did not impact the recorded book value of the loans, but impacted the earnings capacity of these loans. In fact, if the bank were to divest these loans, the value they would fetch would reflect the earnings they are expected to generate. The interest rate changes typically do not affect the value of the loans recorded on the balance sheet—the value of the loan expected to be repaid equals the amount to be lent and is not affected by changes in interest rates, unless the change in interest rate affects the probability of repayment. If interest changes were to affect the repayment of the loans, then the economic value as well as the accounting value of the loans would change as well. The focus here lies on where the change in interest rate affects the bank: the change in interest rates affects the earnings of the bank and thus its economic value and its equity value.

Note that if the deposit rate increased by 1%, income would drop to USD 4.2 million and the value of the perpetual cash flows would drop to USD 84 million. This implies a 16% drop in equity value for a 1% change in the deposit rate. If the increase in deposit rates were associated with an increase in the equity discount rate, the value would drop even lower.

The example suggests a type of static analysis that ignores risk in NII and its impact on future income volatility and equity value. Ironically, as NII becomes more stable, the forecasted earnings stream of the bank resembles a fixed rate bond, and the present value of that bond fluctuates with interest rates. If a bank were able to create NII in a way that was proportional to short-term rates, it could instead create an income stream resembling a floating rate bond, whose payments were uncertain but whose value was stable.

ALM Policy	Impact on Income	Impact on Equity
Stabilize NII	Stable	Risky
Stabilize value	Variable	Stable

FIGURE 1.8   Bank's Objectives

The emphasis a bank places on either of the two closely related yet sometimes competing objectives depends on many factors, including

- The ability of the bank to sustain fluctuations in net income
- The bank's tolerance for earnings fluctuations
- The bank's sensitivity to balance sheet ratios
- Shareholder preferences and peer group or competitive pressures

Since the bank's equity is the difference between its assets and liabilities, most banks will try to balance the risk profile of the assets and liabilities using ALM. By doing this, equity cash flows are less exposed to fluctuations in interest rates. Whether the bank at that point seeks to stabilize earnings or stabilize value is a matter of bank policy and preference.

Fluctuations in Net Income
A bank's net interest income fluctuates as interest rates change, loans come due, deposits are withdrawn, and new loans are funded. Accordingly, there is a risk that the bank may not be able to cover operating expenses. In a highly volatile interest rate environment, particularly when the level, slope, and curvature of the yield curve changes, the impact on earnings can be substantial, and can quickly erode the bank's net interest rate margin. While a bank may be able to sustain an operating deficit for a short period of time, prolonged shortfalls will lead to financial distress for the bank. For this reason, NII stabilization is usually considered the most important aspect of ALM whenever unmanaged NII volatility is too great.

To stabilize the net income, a bank can shift the source of its earnings from interest-rate sensitive sources to less interest-rate sensitive sources. The primary examples are fees banks charge for underwriting loans, extending different types of credit, and providing services to customers, such as trust, asset management, and trading.

Fluctuations in Earnings

If earnings were the same as income, the issues would be the same. However, accounting rules that require banks to mark various assets and liabilities to market cause fluctuations in the values of assets and liabilities, which must be reported into earnings. For instance, traded assets and liabilities need to be marked-to-market to reflect their fair value. This may be easy to accomplish when the assets are widely traded, reliable price information is available, and markets behave normally, but may be more difficult when price information is less readily available or less reliable.

Variable earnings can lead to unwelcome fluctuations in share value if shareholders make incorrect inferences about value due to reported earnings fluctuations. Also, reduced share value may make it more difficult for banks to grow by acquisition, since the value of their shares as currency in the marketplace is lower.

Sensitivity to Balance Sheet Ratios

Balance sheet ratios based on book values are usually greatly affected by changes in interest rates. However, fluctuations in market-value based ratios (such as the market value of debt-to-equity ratio) can be affected profoundly by interest rate changes. In counterparty trading, the requirements for the bank to post collateral depend on the strength of its financial statements. Also, in the various loans to the bank, lines may not be renewed due to adverse balance sheet changes. Balance sheet ratios can affect loan covenants, trigger collateral clauses, and cause credit ratings changes. Therefore, if a bank is close to violating a balance sheet constraint, it may run the risk of increasing its operating costs due to increased collateral requirements, and higher interest rates on new debt.

Shareholder Preferences and Peer Group or Competitive Pressures

Shareholders may expect banks to have similar risk profiles, and therefore they might reward banks to the extent that their risk profiles resemble those of their peers. For example, if all banks stabilized NII, value fluctuations would affect all banks in the same way, causing no surprises for shareholders. Investors could then be indifferent between choosing which banks to invest in. When banks deviate materially from the risk management practices of their peers, they risk having their share price discounted.

1.6 Limit Structure For On- and Off-Balance Sheet Exposures

Banks possess a bewildering array of "limits" to keep exposures under control. These are organized in a matrix-hierarchy hybrid structure and most limits are an amalgam of at least two elements of exposure.

Some limits are oriented toward managing exposures taken by individual traders or desks overall. Few bankers outside the Treasury and dealing room areas have single-handed authority to bind their bank legally to transactions. Even very senior bankers do not have personal sign-off authority on loans, for example, except up to some small amount. Sometimes two or more senior directors can sign off on medium-sized credits, but generally procedure has to be followed, with appropriate applications directed to the credit risk department, which then processes the application on 1) merit, 2) credit portfolio suitability, and 3) profitability (usually in that order). Specific customers of a bank will have been allocated a credit limit. This credit limit is often not communicated to the customer, to avoid customers engaging in shopping between banks.

Other limits are counterparty credit exposure limits. These limits are focused on one customer at a time and are intended to capture the credit aspects of all types of transactions that the bank conducts with that customer, not only loans.

There are also limits that are market risk focused and these ensure the bank keeps control of exposures in the trading book.

Off-balance sheet exposures are generally converted into on-balance sheet "loan equivalents" for credit risk purposes and into "factor equivalents" for market risk purposes. Exposures are then transposed onto the relevant limits for inclusion in overall portfolio management.

Finally, some limits have an operational focus. For example, it is common for large banks to experience "failed" trades. Most of these are for small values and are incorporated in specific data gathering processes for operational risk. On occasion, a large settlement may fail, leading to immediate management intervention and loss control. The maximum amount of settlement-fail exposure that can pass without management intervention is defined as the "Exception Limit" for that type of settlement.

1.6.1 Value Limits

Value limits are common in both credit risk management and market risk management. Within credit risk management a credit limit signals the largest monetary exposure the bank is willing to take on a credit-risky counterpart. Within market risk management, a factor limit indicates the largest exposure the bank is willing to be exposed to for that factor.

One such factor limit is Present Value of 1 bp change in yield (PV01). This is a popular duration-based measure of interest rate risk, which can be observed not only per position, but also on a net portfolio basis.

Other factor limits are: Convexity (for fixed income positions), Delta, Gamma, Theta, Vega, and Rho (for option positions) and CS01 (for traded credit risk positions).

An example of non-factor value limits are: Asset/Liability repricing/roll-over concentration, gap-to-asset ratios, gap-to-equity ratios and absolute limits on the net gap (for ALM Gap management).

1.6.2 Time Limits

Limit structures are normally based on volume or value. However, it does make sense to consider the risk of loss across time horizons, rather than solely as an instantaneous value. This, ultimately, leads to the presence of time in the hierarchy of limits in a modern bank.

Intraday vs. Overnight
Banks are forced to decide what to do with exposures that last for more than a day. This is reflected in the design of limits, with banks making the distinction between intraday and overnight limits.

Intraday limits, as the name suggests, are in place during the business day. It is a basic assumption that desks with intraday limits will have somebody in charge during the day. As a result, such limits have higher value than their overnight equivalents.

Overnight limits are lower than intraday limits, as staff are not at work during the overnight time slot. That makes the overnight limit a sort of passive caretaker, designed to limit losses should overnight financial market volatility on the other side of the Earth flare up between two business days.

A dealer coming to the end of a trading day must look to unwind or hedge exposure, so the remaining exposure can fit under the more restrictive overnight limit. The trading exposure can then be put on again the following morning.

Larger banks with dealing capacity in multiple time zones can make use of a different strategy to take advantage of larger intraday limits: rolling the book. Rolling the book entails one office handing over and signing off on either the gross or the net limit utilization, together with further management instructions, at the end of the business day, to the office in the following financial center. For foreign exchange, by way of example, this could mean the Singapore desk handing over to the London desk during the London morning and London desk handing over to New York desk in the London afternoon.

This limit type is relevant to FX and money market traders and their books.

Maturity and Duration

It is common for banks to use time limits for interest rate sensitive positions. Fixed income bonds and fixed rate loans are both sensitive to changes in yield-to-remaining-maturity and it is a long-established fact that long duration sensitivity is more pronounced than short duration sensitivity in such instruments. It therefore makes sense for banks to impose a maximum time limit on positions in various instruments that are exposed to interest rate risk. This comes in the form of maximum maturities for government bonds, interest rate swaps, short-term interest rate, and bond futures. These limits are usually further subdivided into currencies.

This limit type is relevant to interest rate traders and their books.

Credit Horizon

Although credit limits are examples of value limits, it is vital to include a time element as well. For example, consider the credit curve, i.e., the two-dimensional plot of CDS spreads over time. This curve is normally upward sloping, suggesting that longer-term credit risk is more sensitive than shorter-term credit risk. In other words, credit risk for the same name is greater for longer exposures than it is for shorter exposures.

Banks organize credit limits by time band. A typical bank may have limits of up to five years on credits for high quality corporates, but perhaps just two-year limits for high quality banks. At the same time such a bank may have a two-year limit on low quality corporates and a limit of only six months (or maybe zero) on low quality banks.

This limit type is relevant to treasury managers, bankers, relationship managers, and credit officers, and to their books.

RSA and RSL

The value of rate sensitive assets (RSA) fluctuates up (down) in value as interest rates move down (up), and up (down) in future income as interest rates move up (down).

Rate sensitive liabilities (RSL) behave the exact opposite way.

Banks are therefore focusing on the gap between RSA and RSL at different time points (buckets). A bank following a matched funding policy will have very small or non-existent gaps, while banks actively mismatching funding and lending will have positive or negative gaps, depending on strategy.

A zero gap means a bank's net interest income is insulated from interest rate risk, while positive and negative gaps leave it open to interest rate risk. Successfully managing this risk is at the heart of Asset and Liability Management.

This limit type is relevant to Treasury traders and ALM managers.

1.6.3　Volatility Limits

Volatility Limits

When pricing and valuing positions using implied volatility, banks implement volatility limits.

For example, if a bank has sold options outright or sold instruments with embedded short option positions, the value of those options will fall with a corresponding rise in implied volatility. Although the volatility exposure can be hedged in the market, banks keep track of their net volatility exposure through actively maintaining volatility limits.

Volatility estimations based on end-of-day closing prices are sufficient for many markets, but some markets are so volatile that intraday volatility calculations are required. The market for options on foreign exchange is an example of such a market.

Value-at-Risk (VaR) Limits

A VaR limit for a trader or a book is an allocated limit identifying the maximum VaR exposure the trader or book is allowed to maintain. When moving from VaR calculations for a single position to VaR calculations for multiple positions, or a book, the inter-asset correlation coefficient is taken into account. When the correlation used in a VaR calculation is equal to 1, it follows that the sum of the VaRs of all subportfolios is equal to the total VaR for the organization as a whole.

For this reason, some banks choose not to diversify VaR across major risk classes, such as interest rates, FX, equities, commodities, and credit. Their VaR allocation to individual business lines is strictly a weighted average proportion of the overall group VaR.

Other banks choose to diversify VaR across business lines using actual correlation coefficients. As correlation coefficients are usually less than 1, the sum of all business line VaRs is normally larger than reported overall group VaR.

Most banks adopt a top-down approach to VaR limit setting.

When the correlation coefficients are assumed to be 1, this is a straightforward carving out of the group VaR to allocate to business units.

In the second instance above, when the correlation coefficients are not assumed to be 1, banks need to continuously calculate central group VaR taking multiple daily market changes into account, and then reverse the group VaR calculation to arrive at each business unit VaR. This is a cumbersome process, which is most often solved by allocating a conservative proportion of correlation scaled group VaR to each risk class and then letting traders and business line managers try to optimize subportfolio VaRs to meet the hard business line VaR limit. This may be more capital efficient in the long run, but comes with a significant operational risk dimension.

1.6.4 Gross Position versus Net Limits

Banks that focus mostly, or only, on net limits sometimes wake up to unpleasant surprises.

Net limits, by their very nature, report a small exposure as a result of two larger exposures, one long and the other short, balancing or netting each other out. This is typical of exposure books that are allowed to contain both long and short positions. As all books have exposure limits and, because unused limit room is capital inefficient for a bank, it follows that net exposure books do reach the net limit regularly.

This is not a problem when the net exposure is large in relation to the gross individual exposures in the book (say, over 80%). However, there are certain situations where this may hide a significant risk:

1. When net exposure is small or very small when compared to the gross exposures (say, less than 2%)
2. When either the long or the short gross exposure is fictitious or nonexistent, as seen in cases of fraud

In the first case, if the long/short pair(s) in the book display a correlation of less than +1, changes to this correlation could find the book simultaneously losing both on the short and on the long position. Full positive correlation (+1) is only possible for trades in the same instrument, while even insignificant differences in the two positions leads to less than perfect positive correlation.

In the second case, if a trader can influence book positions without executing real trades, the trader can appear to be exposed to less market risk in limit control reports than is really the case. Société Générale trader Jerome Kerviel simultaneously had access to middle office and front office systems of the bank. The bank did not discover the problem—a real long position on EuroStoxx and Dax futures was balanced by fictitious short positions—until it had lost EUR 4.9 billion in January 2008. This loss was as a result of a 10% drop in European stock markets that month, revealing Kerviel's fictitious short position.

In both the first and second cases it is clear that the likelihood of intervention would have been very high if knowledge of the gross positions in addition to the net book positions were reported and understood.

Net positions deal mostly with regulatory requirements, while gross positions can expose imbalances in the economic realities for a bank. Both are important to grasp and banks need to have not only limits on net exposure, but also limits on gross exposure.

1.7 Summary

This chapter has introduced a number of key concepts and issues involved in organizing the asset and liability management function.

The Role of the Treasury
■ Regardless of business model, the Treasury of a bank is the heart of its operations—all cash flows in the bank will go through the Treasury at one time or another.

Treasury Risk
■ Treasury risk is measured in interest rate and in foreign exchange terms. Interest rate risk is measured in basis points, or one-onehundredth of a percent or 0.01%, while FX risk is measured in pips, which are typically value changes in the fourth decimal point of the FX quotation.

- Internal controls play a crucial role in catching and mitigating risks in Treasury before they can have any significant negative effect on the organization. The list of control points is rather long, as can be seen from the sample shown in Figure 1.2.

Asset and Liability Management Committee (ALCO) Activities

- The activities of the Asset and Liability Management Committee are varied, but they start with making sure the asset mix and liability mix on the balance sheet are in accordance with approved Board policies. The day-to-day work of the ALCO consists of sub-optimizing the two mixes to maximize the difference between asset income and liability expense, the Net Interest Income (NII).
- Although the NII can theoretically be increased to very attractive levels, it cannot be done without incurring liquidity risk. A well-functioning ALCO will ensure that liabilities are spread over a wide range of funding sources and make sure that holding periods for assets are not jeopardized by unexpected asset illiquidity.
- ALCO reports outline asset/liability mismatches/gaps and quantify the risks incurred.

Board Policies for ALM and ALCO

- Board ALM policies need to be sufficiently prescriptive to preempt Treasury managers taking excessive risks, yet at the same time flexible enough that Treasury can position the bank to avoid any market related problems that may occur.
- ALM policies must include guidelines for the asset/liability mix overall and per division, as well as pricing, term, and maturity guidelines.

Asset and Liability Management (ALM) Risk

- Changes in asset income and liability cost can be small and the difference between them can appear insignificant over time. However, the NII is often a major source of economic value of a bank and so has a direct influence on the value of the bank's own equity. Good ALM risk management is therefore very detailed and must react quickly to even insignificant market changes.

Limit Structure for On- and Off-Balance Sheet Exposures

- Banks operate vast matrices of limits to ensure that ALM policies are not jeopardized by deliberate or accidental exposure excesses caused by dealers, the markets, or both.

- Limits are commonly either value limits, time limits, or volatility limits.
- Gross position versus net limits must also be in place to avoid catastrophic losses when an apparently acceptable net risk position turns into disaster, when it is discovered that one side of a long/short portfolio is fictitious, or non-existent, such as with Société Générale in January 2008.

CHAPTER 2

Interest Rate Risk
in the Banking Book

In this chapter, we focus on how banks manage the interest rate risk in their banking book, i.e., the risk related to non-traded assets and liabilities such as loans and deposits. The interest rate risk in the banking book differs from credit or default risk: it relates to the impact interest rate changes may have on the value of the loans and deposits, and by extension, the overall earnings and the value of the bank.

On completion of this chapter the reader will have an improved understanding of:

- The nature of interest rate risk in the banking book: how it affects net interest income and bank equity
- How interest rate risk is measured and managed in the banking book
- Strengths and weaknesses of Duration Gap models used to manage ALM market risk

2.1 Net Interest Income Risk In The Banking Book

Net interest income (NII) is exposed primarily to market risk and secondarily to credit risk. Market risk arises from changing interest rates and the repricing of assets and liabilities. The remainder of the section will discuss the impact interest rate changes have on the earnings and value of the bank, or the interest rate in the banking book. Credit risk results from customers defaulting on their loans, which then reduces the bank's earning assets. To understand market risk in the banking book, it is best to begin with a simplified example.

EXAMPLE

HPBank offers its retail customers balloon mortgages at fixed interest rates that reset every five years. A balloon mortgage does not fully amortize, so that a large principal payment (balloon) must be made at maturity.The balloon mortgage is often replaced with a new balloon mortgage at a repriced rate. The reset feature gives customers a mortgage at a fixed repayment rate for a significant period and has proven to be popular.

HPBank does not take customer deposits on a similar basis. Most of its deposits have a very short contractual maturity. For example, deposits that may be withdrawn on demand or after 30 days' notice are the bank's most common deposit product. As a result, the bank pays a one-month market rate for these deposits.

HPBank is running a business that has a significant amount of interest rate risk. It is receiving the fixed five-year rate from its mortgage customers and paying the one-month rate to its depositors. Unless HPBank's Treasury manages this risk in the wholesale financial markets, if interest rates rise across the yield curve, the bank will have to pay more for its deposits within a period of at most 30 days, but will not be able to increase all its mortgage rates for up to five years.

The actual cost to HPBank will greatly depend on the average time to the repricing of the mortgages. For older mortgages with a short time to maturity, the HPBank will just have to wait that short time until it can refinance at a higher rate. However, for newer mortgages with a long time to maturity, the HPBank will have to wait that long time until it can refinance at a higher rate.

The dangers of not managing interest rate risk in the banking book were highlighted in the example of the American savings and loan crisis in the early 1990s.

EXAMPLE

In the US, savings and loan associations (S&Ls) are essentially mortgage lenders, with the ability in some US states to make direct investments in other businesses and carry out property development.

Estimating the total cost of the bailout of the S&Ls is difficult, but some reports put the figure as high as USD 500 billion. Although there were instances of fraud, the root cause of the disaster was twofold.

First, mortgages were issued on properties with greatly inflated prices. When the property market collapsed the collateral value for many mortgages was erased. Second, although interest rates on a large number of mortgages were fixed, many mortgages were "callable," that is, they had a prepayment provision so that customers could repay the mortgages early without paying a penalty, enabling them to refinance their mortgages at a lower cost when interest rates started to fall. Unfortunately, the S&Ls were still locked into paying higher interest rates on financing for the original mortgages.

This mismatched position of being locked into paying a higher rate for funds, with the only source of income being new mortgages issued at lower rates, caused many S&Ls to collapse, with losses of billions of dollars.

Until the 1980s, S&Ls were mainly mutual associations owned by their members. However, as a result of the "S&L Crisis," they are now primarily owned by the US government or by stockholders.

2.1.1 Basic NII Risk Model

In ALM terminology, assume HPBank's USD 200 million mortgage loan portfolio reprices every five years at LIBOR + 2% and its USD 180 million in deposits reprice every month at LIBOR − 1%. Its rate sensitive assets (RSA) are the mortgages it holds, or USD 200 million. Its rate sensitive liabilities (RSL) are its deposits, or USD 180 million. HPBank's repricing gap is defined to be the difference between its rate sensitive assets and its rate sensitive liabilities in a given time bucket. The cumulative gap is the running sum of the periodic gap measures.

For convenience, assume that a constant fraction of the mortgages (i.e., 20%) mature every year and are replaced with new mortgages. Also assume that while some depositors come and go every month, the level of deposits stays the same.

In this case, if three-month LIBOR goes up by 1% (so it affects both mortgage rates and deposit rates), we can expect asset income to rise by 20 basis points in the next year, as only 1/5 of the assets will reprice. The following table shows the repricing schedule for assets and liabilities assuming deposit repricing is effectively instantaneous.

	Year					
	0	**1**	**2**	**3**	**4**	**5**
Rate sensitive assets — RSA						
Balloon mortgages	0	40	40	40	40	40
Rate sensitive liabilities — RSL						
Deposits	180					
Repricing gap	−180	40	40	40	40	40
Cumulative gap	−180	−140	−100	−60	−20	20

FIGURE 2.1   Repricing Gap Analysis

An asset-sensitive bank will show a positive cumulative gap, and a liability-sensitive bank will show a negative cumulative gap. An asset-sensitive bank benefits from rising rates, while a liability-sensitive bank is hurt by rising rates.

The table suggests HPBank is liability-sensitive and will therefore be hurt by rising interest rates. Taken at face value in Year 0, HPBank's repricing assets are worth USD 0 and its liabilities USD 180 million, so its gap is −USD 180 million. This implies that a 1% rate increase now has no impact on mortgage income, but increases the cost of deposits by 1% or USD 1,800,000. Therefore, every 1% increase in interest rates affects NII adversely by USD 1,800,000 in year zero. In Year 1, 20% of the mortgages reprice, so the additional 1% yield is earned on 20% of the mortgage portfolio. By the end of Year 2, 40% have repriced, and so forth until Year 5, when there is yet again balance between income and expense.

On a present value basis, the 1% increase in interest rates would therefore have a devastating effect on the value of HPBank's equity.

In practice, even the simplest bank would have a much more complicated repricing gap analysis table. However, we have kept the analysis simple to focus on the methodology without being overwhelmed with the details of the repricing structure of all of a bank's assets and liabilities.

2.1.2 Basic NII Risk Management

The bank could reduce its exposure to rising interest rates by doing one of the following:
- Reducing the average repricing time of its loans
- Increasing the average repricing time of its deposits
- Entering into interest rate swaps

Practically speaking, the first two options may be difficult. These options are structural hedges or balance sheet hedges where the bank changes its overall asset and liability composition. The first could be accomplished by offering adjustable-rate mortgages instead of fixed-rate mortgages, but the bank might find the demand for its mortgages is lower as a result. The second could be accomplished by offering depositors certificates of deposit (CDs) with higher rates for longer deposit terms, but most depositors prefer to keep their accounts liquid, and available immediately. In addition, the higher interest rates paid will affect profitability.

The third option is an example of a financial hedge. Here the bank could enter into an interest rate swap agreement wherein it would receive floating payments and pay fixed payments. In this type of swap arrangement, the increased payments of the swap would offset the losses to NII. Conversely, when NII was high because of falling rates, HPBank would have higher compensating NII income.

Hedging with Interest Rate Swaps

Continuing with the HPBank example, suppose the bank were to enter a fixed-for-floating interest rate swap linked to LIBOR, i.e., pay fixed interest in exchange for floating interest at Time 0. In particular, the swap would be structured as five swaps, each swap with a USD 40 million notional amount, and maturities ranging from one to five years.

The logic of this approach is to take the fixed payments on the mortgages and replace them with an index-linked equivalent. Also, since each swap can be represented as selling a fixed rate bond and buying a floating rate bond (see Chapter 3 in the *Market Risk Management* book for further detail on this analogy), it is simple to incorporate into the repricing table:

	Year					
	0	**1**	**2**	**3**	**4**	**5**
Rate sensitive assets — RSA						
Balloon mortgages	0	40	40	40	40	40
Swap floating side	200					
Rate sensitive liabilities — RSL						
Deposits	180					
Swap fixed side		40	40	40	40	40
Repricing gap	20	0	0	0	0	0
Cumulative gap	20	20	20	20	20	20

FIGURE 2.2   Repricing Gap Analysis with Swap

The result looks appealing, completely eliminating the repricing gap. However, while the interest rate swap is the simplest and most popular ALM management tool, it has its own problems. As discussed in Chapter 3 of the *Market Risk Management* book in the GARP FRR series, the swap creates counterparty risk and margining risk, which may be difficult for HPBank to manage. Also, if the NII risk model assumptions are incorrect, a swap may overhedge or underhedge the risk.

For example, suppose that rates dropped and many mortgages refinanced. If twice as many mortgages refinanced in the first year than were expected, and the remaining evenly distributed mortgages refinanced on schedule, the resulting Repricing Gap Analysis would show:

	Year					
	0	**1**	**2**	**3**	**4**	**5**
Rate sensitive assets — RSA						
Balloon mortgages	0	80	30	30	30	30
Swap floating side	200					
Rate sensitive liabilities — RSL						
Deposits	180					
Swap fixed side		40	40	40	40	40
Repricing gap	20	40	−10	−10	−10	−10
Cumulative gap	20	60	50	40	30	20

FIGURE 2.3 Repricing Gap Analysis with Swap After Rates Collapse

The positive cumulative gap shows that the bank was not hedged with the plain vanilla interest rate swap; rather, it overhedged because it assumed no refinancing (i.e., repayments) of the mortgages. Ironically, the simple hedge moved the bank from being liability-sensitive to being asset-sensitive.

2.1.3 Critiques of the Basic NII Risk Model

There are four major critiques of the basic NII risk model, most of which can be addressed using more advanced models. None of them completely eliminates model risk or the risk of over- or underhedging NII risk. The major critiques are concerned with differential interest rate sensitivities, the calculation of effective repricing dates, the lack of a link to the amount of funds intermediated and the lack of measurement of change in market value. These are all explained below.

Differential Interest Rate Sensitivities

Assets and liabilities of the same repricing period do not necessarily have the same sensitivity to interest rate changes. For example, if mortgage rates are linked to one interest rate index and deposit rates do not have a one-to-one relationship, or correlation, to interest rate changes, a model that treats the interest rate sensitivities as being the same will misstate the NII interest rate risk. For instance, many banks price their loans off a prime rate pricing grid, where the credit quality of the customer affects the margin paid above or below that prime rate. A high-rated customer with lower default risk would pay below prime rate and a low-rated customer, with a higher default risk, would pay a premium above the prime rate. Deposits, on the other hand, are priced either off the interbank market for the larger banks or off the local interest rate levels for smaller banks. As large banks compete for large corporate and other institutional deposits, these deposits are often priced close to what other larger banks pay in the interbank market. Thus, changes in the deposit rates offered by the larger banks often reflect yield changes in the interbank market. Smaller banks that are less able to compete for institutional deposits and rely more on retail deposits and smaller corporate deposits for their funding, often price their deposits in competition with other smaller banks.

This problem is normally addressed using historical regression analysis to determine the relationship between asset rates and interest rates, and between deposit rates and interest rates. However, as bank strategies change, the relationship between earning assets and funding liabilities, including the earnings spread changes, may provide incorrect results.

Also, rate sensitivities at different maturities will almost certainly differ. For example, a given change in the three-month LIBOR rate will have a different effect on short-term deposit rates and long-term time deposit and CD rates. This problem can be addressed by estimating the historical impact of three-month LIBOR on the two rates in question, or using a different, more long-term, index base to model the pricing structure.

Effective Repricing Dates

As we saw in the earlier HPBank example, although a five-year fixed rate mortgage that converts to an adjustable mortgage has a maximum repricing period of five years, its expected repricing period is shorter due to the possibility of prepayment. If customers repaid their loans randomly, this would not create problems for large banks, but in fact, customers repay their loans more frequently when interest rates fall, because they can secure alternative financing at a lower cost. For a bank, which normally would benefit from falling rates, this could be a disaster: the repricing period of the assets falls precisely when interest rates fall, prompting increasing early repayments, further weakening the bank's NII.

Banks combat the weakening NII, due to interest rate changes, differently. One widely used approach is to penalize those borrowers who want to repay their loans early. As long as the penalty is substantial enough and is enforceable, the incentive for borrowers to refinance at a lower cost is reduced or prohibited on economic grounds. Another alternative is to extend the loans with terms that clearly prohibit early repayment of the loan, or allow only partial early repayment of loans.

Deposits have the opposite tendency. While contractually, depositors are not required to keep liquid funds on deposit for very long, in fact, they tend to leave their deposits for longer periods of time, even if interest rates rise and the bank does not raise its deposit interest rate. This phenomenon is called deposit "stickiness." These deposits are considered to be the bank's "core deposits" and play an important function in the funding of the bank. As these core deposits are not sensitive to interest rates and are kept in the bank for extended time periods, correctly identifying these deposits and assessing their size is one of the important pieces of analysis a successful ALM function does.

The effective repricing period for HPBank's deposits may turn out to be a year even though the contractual repricing period is a month. If this is the case, HPBank would temporarily benefit from increases in interest rates if it kept its deposit rate the same while enjoying higher income on its repriced loans. However, if the bank does this for a long time, it can expect to see erosion in its depositor base.

Typically, larger commercial deposit customers and more sophisticated retail deposit customers move their deposits to accounts that momentarily earn higher yields. Once these depositors start to move their core deposits on a large scale, the bank should counter by offering more competitive rates to these customers. Often, relatively higher interest rates offered on larger and longer maturity time deposits reduce these customers' yield-maximizing behavior.

Link to Amount of Intermediated Funds

The simple NII model treats assets and liabilities as if the amounts were unaffected by changes in interest rates. However, as we saw in the last paragraphs, changes in rates affect the number of loans outstanding and the amount of deposits held. To estimate the bank's true NII sensitivity to interest rate changes, it is necessary to consider the impact of rate changes on the size of assets and liabilities.

The complexity lies in the diverging direction of the two feedback loops. Lower interest rates fuel increasing lending activity, which, given the bank's capital position, can increase the bank's earning assets. Lower interest rates can also fuel early repayments, particularly of retail loans. These early repayments reduce earning assets, the yield on earning assets, and the net interest margin. Lower interest rates also reduce the risk that borrowers will default. Finally, lower interest rates reduce the bank's funding costs.

Higher interest rates lead to higher earnings yield for the bank, but with attendant higher costs to fund its assets. Higher interest rates reduce the incentives of prepayment, but also introduce the risk that financially struggling weak borrowers may not be able to continue to make higher interest payments in a timely manner, leading to defaults and loss of earning assets to follow. Moreover, the higher interest rates could prompt depositors to shift their funds to bank deposits, further increasing the bank's funding costs.

Change in Market Value

The strongest criticism of the NII risk model is that while it considers risk to income, it does not consider risk related to changes in the market values of assets and liabilities as mentioned above. Hence, no ALM risk report is complete without measures of both NII risk and value risk. The changes in market values and earnings capacity ultimately affect the equity value of the bank. This type of risk is often called equity risk, since it has to do with risk to the changes in assets minus liabilities. Equity risk measurement using duration is the subject of the next section.

2.2 Equity Risk In The Banking Book

Although the banking book is largely not marked-to-market, and its value is adjusted to the expected recovery on the loans included in that banking book, historically, risk managers have wanted to know how changes in interest rates impact the net value of the bank's assets and liabilities. The purpose of this exercise is to understand the longer-term impact, outside of short-term earnings fluctuations, of rising or falling rates on the bank.

Because future assets and liabilities are priced to market when they are originated (when loans are underwritten and funded, investment securities purchased, and the deposits made) they are not affected by changes in today's interest rates, but only by the future level of interest rates. Therefore, the focus is on the current portfolio of assets and liabilities to determine how sensitive it is to changes in interest rates. The most widely used tool for this purpose is modified duration, which was introduced in Chapter 3 of the *Market Risk Management* book in the GARP FRR Series. By way of review, the modified duration of a bond is the estimated percentage drop in the value of the bond per 1% rise in yield.

The change in the bank's equity for a change in interest rates can therefore be written as:

$$\Delta E = -[(MD\text{-}a \times V\text{-}a) - (MD\text{-}l \times V\text{-}l)] \times \Delta \bar{r}$$

E	*Equity value of the bank*
MD_a	*Modified duration of assets*
MD_l	*Modified duration of liabilities*
V_a	*Value of assets*
V_l	*Value of liabilities*
$\bar{r}$	*Average yield*

When divided by the value of the assets of the bank, the term in parentheses is known as the duration gap. The duration gap measures the percentage sensitivity of the bank's assets per 1% change in yields.

EXAMPLE

HPBank (above) had USD 200 million in loans and USD 180 million in deposits. If the modified duration of the loans is estimated to be 3, and the modified duration of the deposits is estimated to be 1, then the change in HPBank's equity value per 1% change in yield is:

Change in equity value   = -[(3 x 200) - (1 x 180)] x 1%
                               = -USD 4.2 million per 1% change in yield

The duration gap is [(3 x 200) - (1 x 180)]/200 or 2.1% per 1% change in yield.

2.2.1 Hedging Equity Risk

Equity risk can also be hedged using interest rate swaps. Interest rate swaps, as mentioned above, insulate the bank's NII from certain fluctuations in interest rates. Since the variability of interest rates and NII are both reduced, the residual equity value is stabilized as well. Using interest rate swaps to reduce the effect of interest rate variability is sometimes called immunization.

To reduce the variability of NII, the bank enters into swap positions that make the bank's duration gap equal to zero. That is, after immunization, a bank's equity should in theory not be sensitive to changes in interest rates.

In the case of HPBank above, it would need to enter interest rate swaps where it was paying fixed and receiving floating in order to get its duration to zero. From this point of view, the bank itself looks like a swap position (long fixed assets and short floating liabilities), so to reverse its risk it must take the opposite swap position in the marketplace.

The difference between NII hedging and equity hedging is straightforward. NII hedging matches repricing risk in assets and liabilities to produce a stable income stream. This can be achieved by structural or financial hedges. Equity hedging, if successful, converts the NII cash flows into payments that resemble a floating rate bond, whose present value remains immune to changes in interest rates.

2.2.2 Critiques of the Duration Gap Model

In general, the criticisms of duration as a risk measure apply to criticisms of duration-based gap management. These include the dynamic nature of the calculation, the costs of immunization, errors in the linear model, and basis risk. All of these issues were addressed in Chapter 3 of the Market Risk Management book in the GARP FRR Series, so they are covered only briefly here.

Dynamic Calculation
Duration is not constant and changes as a function of time and as a function of yields. Any duration-matching strategy is necessarily short-term in nature and needs to be adjusted frequently to be effective. The dynamic nature of duration calculation has practical implications. As the various hedges come due—swap contracts mature, assets and liabilities mature to be replaced with new assets and liabilities, the shape and structure of the yield curve shifts—the bank has to roll some of the hedges forward. Herein is the risk that hedges may not be perfectly rolled forward or the cost of hedging may actually exceed its potential benefits, reducing their practical application.

Costs of Immunization
Because of the need to hedge dynamically, the changing hedge position creates trading costs and managerial difficulty as mentioned above. Cheaper strategies may be devised that meet the bank's risk management objectives but are not as costly to execute. However, all trading based strategies inherently assume the risks associated with the need to roll hedges forward.

Errors in the Linear Model

Duration models assume the percentage change in price per 1% change in yield is constant, but this is incorrect, because the price functions are nonlinear. To some extent, this can be corrected using convexity, but this increases dependence on the assumption of parallel shifts in the yield curve, a questionable assumption.

Basis Risk

Yields changes are not uniform. Changes in market rates affect different time buckets differently and they affect asset and liability yields differently. As such, a "beta-adjusted" duration gap that reflected these differences might perform better. For example, if the municipal bond index changes 88 bp for every 100 bp change in LIBOR, the hedge ratios for risks related to municipal bonds ("munis") would be the same as LIBOR hedges, except they are multiplied by 0.88 to reflect the reduced risk of munis.

2.3 Conclusions

While bank Treasuries operate differently in some respects, most take primary responsibility for managing the ALM risk of the bank. This involves drawing a balance between stabilizing net income and stabilizing bank equity value: objectives that often compete with one another.

The main determinant of a bank's sensitivity to interest rate changes is its repricing structure. Asset-sensitive banks reprice their assets quickly, and benefit from rising rates, while liability-sensitive banks reprice their liabilities quickly and benefit from falling rates. A bank's repricing schedule is extremely difficult to determine. Some contractual assets, like mortgages, will vary in size (via prepayment changes) as interest rates change. The same is true of some liabilities, such as deposits, even though those are not contractual in nature. The repricing gap analysis tables presented in this chapter do not begin to approach the complexity of actual bank exposures.

Once the bank has modeled its assets and liabilities, it may choose to alter its exposure to interest rates using structural hedges or financial hedges. Structural hedges require a change in bank strategy to increase or decrease various types of assets or liabilities. Financial hedges are usually complex portfolios of interest rate swaps. Both types of hedges can be costly in terms of execution and in terms of producing undesired consequences.

This chapter has explored the basic problems associated with interest rate risk in ALM, but has not addressed advanced issues related to accounting, incentives, or regulatory capital impact. The student is encouraged to explore this field in greater depth upon completion of this volume.

2.4 Summary

This chapter has introduced a number of key concepts and issues involved in treasury risk management.

NII Risk
- The repricing gap analysis table groups assets and liabilities by expected maturity bucket. Until an asset or liability reprices, i.e., resets its fixed rate to new market rates, it presents interest rate risk.
- The repricing gap is the value (by bucket) of repriced assets minus repriced liabilities.
- The cumulative repricing gap is the running sum of the individual repricing gaps.
- An asset-sensitive bank is one with positive cumulative repricing gaps, while a liability-sensitive bank has negative cumulative repricing gaps.
- A bank can hedge NII risk with plain vanilla interest rate swaps, but runs the risk of over- or under-hedging if the underlying asset and liability repricing schedule changes as rates change.
- The basic NII model is criticized on the basis that (a) assets and liabilities have different interest rate sensitivities, (b) effective repricing dates can be different from contractual repricing dates, (c) the amount of intermediated funds can be a function of interest rate levels and (d) NII risk does not address the impact of changing interest rates on bank equity value.

Equity Risk in the Banking Book
- The change in the equity value of the bank can be estimated using duration of assets and liabilities.
- If a bank wanted to neutralize its equity to changes in interest rates, it could also use interest rate swaps.
- Most banks do not focus primarily on this risk

Duration Gap models
- Other problems are: (a) the duration measure is dynamic, (b) immunization against risk can be costly, (c) the linear model used to estimate duration is approximate and does not reflect large changes in rates, and (d) not all rates rise and fall with interest rate indices.

CHAPTER 3

Liquidity Risk in the Banking Book

In this chapter, we focus on how banks manage liquidity risk, that is, the potential short-term cash demands that can be placed upon banks by depositors, borrowers, the bank's own borrowing activities, trading activities, and counterparty interactions. Liquidity squeezes leave banks vulnerable to potential default on their obligations, and in some cases trigger bankruptcy. Because liquidity demands are difficult to predict in advance, they present an important risk to bank managers. This risk is usually managed by the bank's Treasury as part of the asset and liability management function.

On completion of this chapter the reader will have an improved understanding of:

- Sources and uses of liquidity
- Types and drivers of liquidity risk
- Add-on costs of liquidity risk
- The relationship between liquidity risk and the credit crisis of 2007-9
- Liquidity risk measurement issues
- Liquidity risk management alternatives
- Best practices in liquidity risk management
- Liquidity risk reporting

This chapter focuses on funding liquidity risk: the ability of the bank to fund its obligations when they come due. Funding liquidity risk is different from transactional or trading liquidity risk—the ability to trade in markets without significant price concessions—and from the risk of an increase in a security's bid-offer spread or reduction in market depth for a traded security (which was covered in Chapter 6 of the *Market Risk Management* book in the GARP Risk Series). To meet funding liquidity needs, banks may establish holdings of highly liquid assets that they expect to sell on short notice to raise funds when they need them. Thus the funding liquidity risk can become related to trading liquidity risk, but these two different types of risks are not the same.

3.1 Introduction to Liquidity Risk

Liquidity risk is the risk of not being able to meet obligations when they fall due. The two main day-to-day liquidity obligations that are specific to banks are the ability to fund deposit withdrawals, and the ability to fund loan drawdowns. Apart from these two bank-specific liquidity obligations, banks encounter the standard liquidity obligation of paying their bills and other debts in a contractual and timely manner.

Generally, these issues become problematic for banks when their liquidity requirements are not known in advance. Some liabilities have scheduled repayment amounts and dates and can be predicted easily, but one important liability, future deposit levels, cannot be predicted with certainty. Other liabilities, such as those created by counterparty failure or market risk in leveraged cash or derivative positions, cannot be forecasted accurately and therefore can have a significant effect on liquidity requirements.

Examples of bank-related events that can stress a bank's liquidity include:

- Obligations to fund assets (e.g., mortgages)
- Maturing bank debt
- Unusually large depositor withdrawals (potential precursor to a bank run)
- Nonperforming assets (causing cash shortfalls)
- Exercise of customer put provisions requiring a bank to repurchase assets
- Repurchase agreements
- Futures margins
- Counterparty collateral calls (and failure of counterparties to supply collateral)

In one way or another, all financial institutions faced liquidity problems during the global financial crisis of 2007-2009. The first major failure of a financial institution in the US was Bear Stearns in March 2008. Bear Stearns was not a commercial bank, but an investment bank (or "merchant" bank) and as such faced a broader range of risks than commercial banks, which are more heavily regulated and face a more limited range of risks.[5]

EXAMPLE

"A sudden surge of 'broad cash outflows' from counterparties and customers on Thursday March 13, 2008 forced Bear Stearns to tap JPM Chase and the Federal Reserve for funds to shore up liquidity, the investment bank's chief executive said Friday.

During a hastily convened conference call, CEO Alan Schwartz said the bank continued to have very strong liquidity in the first part of the week, but demands from prime brokerage clients, repo clients, and lenders to cash out late Thursday forced the move. Said CFO Sam Molinaro: 'Counterparties that were providing secured financing against assets were no longer willing to provide financing. We lost a lot of capacity.' At the pace funds were being withdrawn, the firm recognized that there could be continued liquidity demands that would 'outstrip our resources,' said Schwartz."

Eventually, Bear Stearns' resources were outstripped and the bank was bought by JPMorgan Chase in a transaction shepherded by the US Government. Had Bear Stearns been able to meet their exceptional liquidity demands, they would not have been forced to sell their assets to another bank, and would likely still be in business today.

Under ordinary circumstances, liquidity demands are met through the normal course of business. When a bank struggles to meet its obligations, it may use the endogenous liquidity of the assets, the exogenous liquidity of the bank's balance sheet, or the contingent liquidity of another financial institution's balance sheet. These three types of liquidity are explained below.

3.1.1 Types of Liquidity

There are three different concepts of liquidity: endogenous liquidity, exogenous liquidity, and external liquidity.

Endogenous liquidity is the liquidity inherent in the banks' assets themselves. Assets exhibit various forms of endogenous liquidity:

---

5   Vincent Ryan, "Sudden Liquidity Crisis for Bear Stearns," CFO Magazine, March 14, 2008; http://ww2.cfo.com/banking-capital-markets/2008/03/sudden-liquidity-crisis-for-bear-stearns/

- Related to the ability to sell the asset in a liquid market rapidly, and at a bid/offer spread (the difference between the price to the buyer and seller of the asset) that is small and minimally affected by the size of the transaction.
- Related to the maturity of the asset. A loan with a term of one-week has far greater natural liquidity than a 10-year loan.
- Related to the quality of the asset. A 30-year US Treasury bond is more liquid than a 30-year prime mortgage, which, in turn, is typically more liquid than a three-year subprime mortgage.

Typically, government issued or government backed securities exhibit the greatest endogenous liquidity.

Exogenous liquidity (often called funding liquidity) is the liquidity provided by the bank's liability structure to fund its assets and maturing liabilities.

Exogenous liquidity is particularly important when the assets of a bank cannot be readily sold (a situation for many commercial and retail banks). Clearly a bank that makes (illiquid) 10-year loans and funds itself entirely on the overnight interbank market is very vulnerable to any refusal by banks to provide funds. Such a bank would have an extreme mismatch between its asset and liability funding structure, and its funding could dry up immediately.

Liquidity mismatches can cause serious problems, as was highlighted by the crisis at Long-Term Capital Management (LTCM), a US hedge fund (see example below). As a hedge fund, LTCM depended on the endogenous liquidity of its assets to secure financing. It relied on the equity provided by its investors and the funds it was able to source from debt markets. As a hedge fund LTCM was not allowed to raise deposits as banks can, but was able to secure short-term loans from banks and institutional investors, including banks and other hedge funds.

In this case rather than selling the assets it pledged them as collateral against shortdated loans. A period of severe market disruption in September 1998 meant that LTCM was unable to readily sell or pledge assets in order to obtain shorter-term funding. This was because lenders were concerned about the asset values, which were very sensitive to rising interest rates. LTCM was not capable of carrying the assets of its business on its balance sheet because it did not have the necessary funding structure.

EXAMPLE

In September 1998, Long-Term Capital Management (LTCM) was rescued from collapse by 16 major counterparties that had agreed to invest USD 4 billion to enable it to "wind down" its USD 200 billion market exposure in an orderly fashion.[6]

LTCM's capital was mainly provided by banks, permitting the investors to "gear up": that is, borrow money and make massive returns on a small equity basis from comparatively small price movements. Unlike other investment vehicles that could borrow money only to a limited extent, LTCM was able to borrow many times the amount of its own capital, and this ultimately led to its near-collapse.

By August 1998, 75% of LTCM's total notional derivatives exposure of more than USD 1 trillion was in the form of interest rate swaps with some 50 counterparties worldwide, none of whom knew the extent of LTCM's overall exposure. Bear Stearns, the Wall Street firm handling LTCM's settlements, "pulled the plug" on the company initially by calling in a USD 500 million payment that LTCM was unable to meet because of its inability to sell supposedly highly liquid assets, such as foreign government bonds, in such large volumes.

As a direct result of the LTCM crisis many trading businesses now ensure that they have better access to long-term funding through instruments such as committed funding lines (i.e., commercial bank commitments to lend to them).

External liquidity is the noncontractual and contingent capital supplied by investors and other institutions to support the bank in times of liquidity stress. External liquidity can also refer to the "lender of last resort," for example, the liquidity supplied by central banks in times of crisis. This capital is contingent on an unexpected liquidity need and is typically supplied during times of crisis using various approaches that are available to banks, institutions, and the central bank. It may include repos, discount window borrowings, or other approaches to provide liquidity—cash—to banks when prompted by a stress event.

While external liquidity in part relates to the financial strength of the bank, or its exogenous liquidity, in part it also relates to the willingness of third parties to support a bank's liquidity needs. This support can come from lenders or shareholders but it can also come from government sources.

Lenders, including other banks, can provide credit lines that are drawn when needed to meet cash needs. When explicit credit lines don't exist, implicit lines sometimes exist: investors or governments that have a vested interest in rescuing financial institutions have turned out to be the greatest providers of contingent capital to support bank liquidity requirements.

---

6   See http://www.treasury.gov/resource-center/fin-mkts/Documents/hedgfund.pdf

EXAMPLE

Warren Buffett purchased USD 5 billion of preferred shares from Goldman Sachs in September 2008, and acquired additional options as part of the package. This was a source of implicit external liquidity that was contracted in advance. However, the capital was obtained at a high cost (10% interest plus warrants). Had Goldman been able to contract for contingent liquidity in advance, it would likely have been cheaper.

3.1.2 Sources of Liquidity Problems

Liquidity is essentially a short-term problem. Most liquidity problems are caused by short-term unexpected liabilities, but they can also be caused by the funding requirements of long-term liabilities. Liquidity risk therefore arises from (a) the variability in short-term assets and liabilities and (b) the short-term components of long-term assets and liabilities.

EXAMPLE

Many banks use an "originate to distribute" model of mortgage banking. A mortgage is issued, warehoused in the bank, and sold together with other mortgages in a pool. These banks need liquidity to fund mortgages, and this usually comes in the form of cash, warehouse loans, and sale proceeds. They also take the risk that mortgage values drop or the demand for mortgage-backed securities fall. As a result, even though the mortgages are long-term in nature, they create short-term liquidity issues for banks.

On the asset side, securities may default or their values may fall. These types of impairment do not cause liquidity problems; the loss in market value affects the accounting treatment of these securities in the financial statements only. However, there is a very important exception if the impaired security was bought with leverage. To maintain the loan-to-value ratio between the loan and the security acting as collateral for the loan, lenders to the bank making the purchase of the impaired security may make margin calls and demand posting of additional collateral to support the transaction. Also, if the security was used as collateral in a trading position, trading counterparties may make collateral calls, stressing the liquidity of the bank because additional collateral demands are typically met through otherwise liquid securities. This is a vicious cycle: the declining values lead to additional collateral requirements, and then to additional liquidity demands, which in turn lead to further declining asset values, as the following picture illustrates.

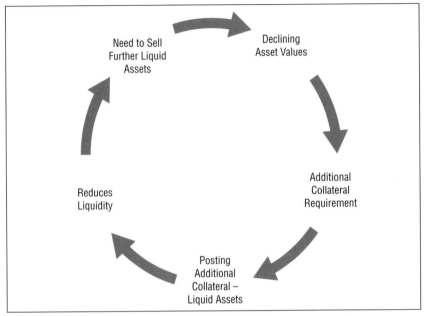

FIGURE 3.1 "Vicious Asset Cycle"

In the case of a commercial bank, when depositors demand their funds, they are converting longer-term bank liabilities into shorter-term liabilities. In a classic "bank run," the short-term liabilities exceed the available liquid assets of the bank, and the bank is forced into liquidating assets, restructuring, or declaring bankruptcy.[7]

Some sources of liquidity risk are not as obvious as loan funding and depositor runs on the bank. A complete liquidity risk assessment would require a bank to examine its repurchase agreements, futures margins, and OTC trading activities to determine if its sources of liquidity and contingent funding are sufficient to meet extreme scenarios.

Repurchase Agreements

A repurchase agreement, or "repo" uses a security as collateral to obtain a loan. The counterparty sells the securities to the lender and agrees to repurchase them at a later date at a fixed price or interest rate formula,

---

7   Arguably, the deposit insurance organizations (such as the FDIC in the US) exist to protect depositors, but they also protect banks by reducing the incentives for depositors to make runs on the bank.

allowing the lender to earn a rate of return on the loan. The loan amount is typically less than the value of the security by a percentage "haircut," which can be quite small for government securities or quite large for very risky securities.

Repos behave like margin loans except that the implicit leverage is much greater. Because the lender takes significant risk in these transactions, it reserves the right to change the interest rate formula, the amount of the haircut, or other credit terms to increase its margin calls when the lender feels it is appropriate. For example, the lender may reserve the right to increase margin calls if a counterparty's credit rating declines. Collectively, these features can lead to rapidly rising liquidity demands in times of financial distress.

EXAMPLE

A bank enters a short-term repo transaction whereby it sells USD 100 million in CDOs with the agreement to repurchase the CDOs with interest. Because of the risk of the instruments, the counterparty normally applies a 20% haircut, so that the bank is able to effectively borrow USD 80 million. As the value of CDOs fell during the credit crisis, haircuts for CDOs increased, and some counterparties would not lend at all on CDOs. Both of these events could dramatically affect a bank's availability of funds.

Futures Margins

Banks often trade on futures exchanges to reduce their market risk and counterparty credit risk. Market risk is reduced by taking hedge positions, and credit risk is reduced by transacting with a well-capitalized exchange. However, in giving up market and credit risk, the bank assumes a great deal of liquidity risk in its futures contracting activities. Since cash demands must be met on a one-day notice,[8] banks can find themselves scrambling for funds, faced with the prospect of liquidating a losing position, selling other assets to raise cash, or finding other sources of short-term liquidity. Failing these remedies, banks could go bankrupt as a result of their hedging operations.

Futures margins may vary with prices, but exchange margin requirements can also change unexpectedly, either for individual contracts or for futures portfolios. This is an additional source of risk to futures hedgers and speculators alike.

---

8   As we saw in Chapter 2 of the *Market Risk Management* in the GARP FRR Series, futures margining requires a daily calculation and settlement of the trade profit or loss.

OTC Collateral Calls

Over-the-counter derivative positions that move against a counterparty in excess of their credit lines usually require collateral to be posted. They can behave like futures margins when the derivative positions resemble futures contracts. They can also behave like repurchase agreements in some cases. Therefore, all the liquidity risks affecting repos and futures apply to OTC contracts as well.

Simply put, nearly all of the bank's assets and liabilities have some liquidity risk associated with them. Some liquidity risks are predictable and well-known in advance, while other risks are unknown in both time and size. This can lead in some cases to incredible cash demands on the bank. If a bank is otherwise healthy, an increase in cash demands can be met by additional short-term borrowing. However, if many banks experience difficulties at the same time, the reduction in available funds to all banks can have disastrous consequences, as happened in 2008-9.

3.1.3 Costs of Mismanaging Liquidity Risk

Liquidity risk extends beyond the potential inability to fund obligations. When a bank's sources of liquidity dry up, the bank may not be able to continue operating without external assistance. When a bank has to sell its assets or go bankrupt, it incurs many add-on losses, including:

- The discount accepted by the bank for selling its assets in a "fire sale"
- The increased cost of funding liabilities in a financially distressed situation
- Reduction in the value of reputation, goodwill, and present value of future growth opportunities in the event of financial distress
- The loss of all goodwill and intangible assets (e.g., reputation and customer relationships) in the event of a bankruptcy

The global financial crisis of 2007-2009 demonstrated that even the largest financial institutions were vulnerable to liquidity risk. The table below shows a sample of firms affected by liquidity management problems.

Date	Place	Event
Feb. 2008	UK	Nationalization of Northern Rock
Mar. 2008	US	Collapse of Bear Stearns
July 2008	US	IndyMac Bancorp seized by federal regulators
Sept. 2008	US	Federal takeover of Fannie Mae and Freddie Mac
Sept. 2008	Germany	Commerzbank buys Dresdner
Sept. 2008	US	WaMu seized by US and assets sold to JPMorgan
Sept. 2008	US	Bankruptcy of Lehman Brothers
Sept. 2008	US	Wells Fargo acquisition of Wachovia
Oct. 2008	Iceland	Nationalization of all major banks
Oct. 2008	Netherlands	Nationalization of Dutch part of Fortis
Oct. 2008	US	Merrill Lynch taken over by Bank of America
Nov. 2008	Latvia	Takeover of Parex after run on the bank
Jan. 2009	Belgium	KBC gets state support
Jan. 2009	Ireland	Nationalization of Anglo Irish Bank

FIGURE 3.2: A Sample of Firms Affected by Liquidity Management Problems

While nationalization or bankruptcy is one extreme outcome of poor liquidity management, this table does not list the thousands of financial institutions that were severely impacted by the crisis. Many of these institutions were able to survive through a combination of asset sales, cost cutting, and capital infusion, but nearly all saw their share prices collapse.

Liquidity problems did not begin with the global financial crisis of 2007-2009. According to a special report by Fitch Ratings's Fitch Bank Failures Study 1990-2003, globally banks experienced a cumulative failure rate of 5.52% during the period analyzed. However, the actual cumulative default rate was 0.48%, suggesting that the majority (94%) of these banks were supported or bailed out before they ever defaulted. While this would seem beneficial from the point of view of systemic risk, we can conclude bank managers at failing banks have not done as well; in many cases they were fired or replaced at the time of the bailout.[9]

---

9   Fitch Bank Failures Study 1990-2003; FDIC: https://www.fdic.gov/bank/individual/failed/banklist.html

3.2 Liquidity Risk Measurement

To measure a bank's aggregate liquidity, it is important to model each of the assets and liabilities that make up a bank's balance sheet. Each asset and liability has cash flow impact associated with it—origination, purchase, dividends, coupons, interest, default and redemption, or sale. Some assets and liabilities lend themselves easily to quantitative models, while others are more difficult to model. This section discusses the classic static liquidity analysis, the liquidity ladder, and its extension into probabilistic liquidity models.

3.2.1 Static Model — The Liquidity Ladder

At any point in time, a bank will typically model its liquidity requirements using a liquidity ladder. The liquidity ladder is used by banks for active liquidity management for periods of a few months at most, but some banks also derive longer-term liquidity ladders to identify weaknesses in their liquidity structure.

The liquidity ladder is a statement of cash flow sources and uses. A simple liquidity ladder for a bank one day in the future might be composed as follows:

Day 1		
Sources of Cash	**Use of Cash**	**Net Cash Requirement**
Maturing assets	Maturing contractual liabilities	
Interest receivable	Interest payable	
Asset sales	Deposit runoffs	
Bank's drawdown on credit lines	Customer drawdown of bank lines	
Total sources	**Total uses**	**Net = Sources - Uses**

FIGURE 3.3: A Simple Liquidity Ladder

The liquidity ladder is similar to the framework the bank uses for calculating its duration and repricing gap, with one fundamental difference. The liquidity ladder looks at the timing and the direction of the cash flows, while the framework for the duration gap analysis looks at the valuation points and not at those times when the value of the various assets are realized.

The one-day liquidity ladder considers contractual payment dates of assets and liabilities, but also incorporates clearing and settlement features of all the bank's assets and liabilities. For example, the sale of an asset today would typically lead to cash settlement in the next 2-3 days. If the bank was depending on that cash to meet an obligation today, it would likely end up defaulting.

If a bank discovered its one-day liquidity gap was negative, it could try to shift some of its assets into overnight loans, but this may be difficult if the assets are illiquid or the settlements delayed. For this reason, banks manage their liquidity ladders by looking several days into the future. The summary table might look as follows:

Day(s)	Total sources	Total uses	Net liquidity	Cumulative
1	–	–	–	–
2	–	–	–	–
3–15	–	–	–	–
15+	–	–	–	–

FIGURE 3.4 Liquidity Summary Table

Wherever net liquidity was negative, the bank could shift its assets and liabilities to fill the funding gap.

EXAMPLE

Bank A has USD 1 million in cash and USD 20 million in loans coming due tomorrow with an expected default rate of 2%. The proceeds will be deposited overnight. The bank owes USD 8 million on a securities purchase that settles in two days, and pays off USD 13 million in commercial paper in three days that is not expected to renew. This is Bank A's current liquidity ladder (without overnight lending):

Day(s)	Total sources	Total uses	Net liquidity	Cumulative
1	20.6*	0.0	20.6	20.6
2	0.0	8.0	(8.0)	12.6
3–15	0.0	13.0	(13.0)	(0.4)

* $20.6 = (20 \times 0.98) + 1$

FIGURE 3.5 Bank U Liquidity Ladder (in USD millions)

The Day 1 sources of funds include cash on hand plus expected loan repayments. The cumulative liquidity for Day 3 is negative, showing that the bank should act now to raise an additional USD 400,000 in cash before Day 3.

Critique of the Static Model
The static liquidity ladder provides a useful starting point for liquidity analysis. However, it is not designed for risk analysis. For example, if loans defaulted at a higher-than-expected rate, or depositors withdrew their funds, Bank A in the above example would have had a much worse liquidity outcome. By planning for the expected case, the bank exposes itself to the risk of liquidity shortfalls. Because of the high cost of those shortfalls, the bank needs to look at liquidity on a worst-case basis, not an expected basis.

To accomplish this, banks perform probabilistic analysis on their assets and liabilities to determine the likely and worst case cash requirements. Banks do not necessarily hold enough cash to cover their worst possible liquidity outcomes, but they should have credit lines large enough to cover the contingency of higher than expected liquidity demands.

Like market and credit risk models, probabilistic models of liquidity need to consider the features of all the assets and liabilities, and understand how their liquidity requirements interact to determine liquidity requirements. This is the topic of the next section.

3.2.2 Probabilistic models

We begin by examining the complexity of a number of the assets and liabilities on a bank's balance sheet, and how they are modeled for liquidity reporting purposes. The goal of this section is to help the student understand not only how banks measure liquidity risks of different types of assets or liabilities, but also how those individual risk assessments are combined into an aggregate risk report.

Deposits
Demand deposits may theoretically be withdrawn at any instant, suggesting that deposits present a great liquidity risk. On the other hand, corporations and individuals who use demand deposit accounts (such as checking accounts) exhibit "sticky" behavior, meaning that because of the costs of switching, banks can expect most retail deposits to stay in place in the short term, provided that extreme events do not occur. Additionally, long-term deposits of various formats are not withdrawn frequently and at their

maturity are often rolled over. Collectively, these deposits, together with some of the more permanent demand deposits, are called core deposits and serve as chief funding source for the bank.

On an everyday basis, liquidity trends are easy to predict. Rents and mortgages are typically paid at the beginning of each month, which requires the depositors to have money available to make these withdrawals. Seasonally, chiefly around holidays, large funds might be withdrawn to make purchases. Withdrawals usually increase on Fridays before the weekend, and deposits increase on Mondays as shops and other businesses deposit the weekend's inflows.

Sophisticated longer-term models of deposit retention incorporate historical behavior of different account types with macroeconomic overlays to reflect overall economic conditions such as changes in interest rates and unemployment. Regional banks are also sensitive to the economics of their regions. The balance between time deposits (such as CDs) and demand deposits can also be modeled, and the relationship tends to depend on the same sorts of variables.

The results of these models include short- and long-term deposit level projections together with estimates in the volatility of deposits. These statistics are then used in the portfolio liquidity model to determine the risk attributable to depositor behavior.

Loans
In the case of loans, two types of liquidity demands arise. One relates to the demand for loans: new loans that must be funded. The other relates to defaulting loans, where cash shortfalls can result.

Loan funding liquidity shortfalls can be managed by increasing sources of lending capital or by tightening underwriting requirements to reduce the number of loans funded. However, the latter option reduces profitability and jeopardizes relationships with good borrowers.

Default risk is measured and modeled comprehensively in major banks, and the expected time pattern of default is used to predict liquidity demands. When borrowers default, they put liquidity strains on banks.

Cash and Securities
Cash and liquid securities held as assets usually do not create liquidity risk directly, with the exception of margin calls on leveraged security investments (see the LTCM example above). However, because cash and securities are held as liquidity buffers, it is important to run risk models for the value

of cash assets and securities to determine if they will be sufficient to meet liquidity needs.

Liquidity models for cash and securities can be derived from value-at-risk models, which are discussed in Chapter 5 of the Market Risk Management book in the GARP Risk Series. The VaR model computes the expected worst-case value for the liquid portfolio with a given level of confidence, using historical data. In addition to a basic VaR model, risk models for these instruments should include the correlations to interest rates and other macroeconomic factors so that the model results can be integrated with liquidity risks of other assets and liabilities.

EXAMPLE

Many banks have counterparty trading agreements that call for same-day settlement of mark-to-market variations in their trading values. In this case, a bank could use its value-at-risk model to determine the likely worst-case cash outlay on a given day to any or all of its bank counterparts.

Aggregation

The best liquidity risk models derive liquidity risks for each asset and liability based on common risk drivers. When risks are aggregated in these types of models, it is clear how aggregate interest rates, default rates, and other macroeconomic influences drive the need for additional liquidity.

For example, a downturn in the stock market may simultaneously increase consumers' cash needs and their propensity to default on credit cards. The bank's assets would fall in value, perhaps triggering collateral requirements on loans used to purchase the assets. Finally, if the bank's credit rating fell, its trading counterparts would require additional capital as well.

Given the difficulty of quantifying all these individual effects and cross effects, many banks will conduct stress tests on their liquidity ladders to assess the adequacy of their liquid assets to cover liabilities coming due. Figure 3.6 shows an example from the Risk Institute.[10] In this example, the Day 1 liquidity ladder is shown under normal business conditions, under an institution-specific crisis, and under a general market crisis.

---

10 International Financial Risk Institute, http://ifci.ch/139350.htm

Cash inflows	Normal business conditions (1)	Institution-specific crisis (3)	General market crisis (2)
Maturing assets	100	100	90
Interest receivable	20	20	10
Asset sales	50	60	0
Drawdowns	10	0	5
Total	180	180	105
Cash outflows			
Maturing liabilities	50	50	50
Interest payable	10	10	10
Deposit runoffs	30	100	60
Drawdowns on lending commitments	50	60	75
Total	140	220	195
Liquidity Excess/(Shortfall)	**40**	**−40**	**−90**

FIGURE 3.6: Day 1 of the Maturity Ladder Under Alternative Scenarios (USD millions)

A report like this one is meant to be used to determine whether a bank has sufficient liquid resources to withstand any reasonable liquidity crisis.

3.3 Liquidity Risk Management

Liquidity risk models are only the beginning of liquidity risk management. Liquidity risk management generally requires a detailed contingency plan with both contracted and uncontracted liquidity provision. Contracted liquidity includes changing asset and liability structures to ensure liquidity is available when needed. It also includes credit lines set up by the bank to cover surprise liquidity requirements. Uncontracted provisions include contingency plans developed by the bank to address liquidity shortfalls.

It is important for a bank to plan for liquidity before it gets into financial distress. During a crisis, sources of liquidity can be very expensive, for example, as when Warren Buffett invested in Goldman Sachs' emergency preferred share issuance.

Under normal circumstances, liquidity can be adequately managed by shifting assets and liabilities, obtaining interbank loans, and drawing down credit lines. Under stress conditions, a bank must think aggressively about how it might increase liquidity.

The most common methods to increase liquidity in stress conditions include:

- Issuing securities such as bonds
- Obtaining interbank or government loans
- Obtaining additional credit lines
- Selling or securitizing assets

EXAMPLE

In the 2007 Annual Report, JPMorgan Chase reported that they issued USD 95.1 billion in long-term debt and trust preferred capital debt securities, explicitly not for funding or capital management purposes. In retrospect, this aided their liquidity position tremendously, since these steps were taken before financial markets collapsed completely in 2008.

In 2013 the JPMorgan Chase issued USD 5 billion net of redemptions and maturities,[11] which included the last remaining outstanding amount of USD 5 billion of the above 2007 issuance.

The cash proceeds of these types of offerings increase bank liquidity unless the cash is invested in less liquid assets.

The first three methods of providing liquidity have already been covered. For example, we saw how Goldman Sachs and JPMorgan Chase issued securities as a liquidity management measure. Less attention has been paid to securitization as a way to mitigate liquidity risk, that is, securitization as an alternative to asset sales.

3.3.1 Securitization

Securitization is a method by which banks sell illiquid assets. Technically, securitization of bank assets is the process by which banks—through various intermittent legal entities—issue bonds where:

- The payment of interest and repayment of principal on the bonds depends on the cash flow generated by a "pool" of bank assets, and
- The bank has transferred its legal rights to payment of interest and repayment of principal to the bondholders.

---

11   JP Morgan 2013 Annual Report, p. 171.

When banks create such bond issues they greatly increase the inherent (endogenous) liquidity of the assets that have been securitized. In the absence of securitization a bank could only make the assets liquid by selling them, a process that is likely to be time consuming and expensive and one that will require substantial effort.

EXAMPLE

A bank that has a large number of auto loans would find it prohibitively costly to sell the loans individually to raise cash. However, if the bank packages the auto loans into a securitized vehicle, obtains a credit rating, and sells the low-risk tranche of the portfolio, it effectively turns illiquid loans into a security that can be sold, whether the bank decides to sell the security or not.

In the US, it is common for banks to securitize many of their retail loan assets—mortgages and revolving credit card debt—on a continuous basis, and then hold the assets in securitized form. This removes these loans from a bank's balance sheet by selling them into a specially created entity often called special purpose vehicle or SPV. Through this transaction, the credit risk of these loans is moved into the SPV and as the SPV issues bonds to finance this purchase, the credit risk is ultimately moved to the holders of bonds issued by the SPV.[12] This process makes the retail assets highly liquid and makes a bank's balance sheet easier to manage because:

- Any lack of capital (for example, due to rapid asset growth or as a consequence of bad debt growth) can be accommodated by selling the securitization bonds.
- Any need to diversify credit risk can be accommodated by selling the bank's own securitized bonds (which may be naturally concentrated in a certain geographical location) and buying other bonds which increase diversification.
- Any need for cash liquidity can be accommodated by securitizing assets through various bonds. Because these bonds do not depend on the credit standing of the bank for their value, they are not likely to be affected by any change in depositor or market sentiment towards the bank.

---

12   Depending on the structure of securitization transaction, the credit risk may not be fully shifted from the bank to the investors in the bonds issued by the SPV. How the regulators respond to the structure of the transaction and treat the credit risk transfer from the bank to the investors in the SPV as a result of the complex transaction is essential in understanding the potential for capital relief and liquidity improvement for the bank. Even the simplest of these approaches and transactions can be quite complex.

3.3.2 Broader Management Principles Around Liquidity Risk

Partly in response to the financial crisis, and partly continuing its tradition of advising banks on best liquidity risk management practices, the Bank for International Settlements published *Principles for Sound Liquidity Risk Management and Supervision*[13] in June 2008.

The document states:

> *"The principles underscore the importance of establishing a robust liquidity risk management framework that is well integrated into the bank-wide risk management process. The primary objective of this guidance is to raise banks' resilience to liquidity stress. Among other things, the principles seek to raise standards in the following areas:*

> - *Governance and the articulation of a firm-wide liquidity risk tolerance;*
> - *Liquidity risk measurement, including the capture of off-balance sheet exposures, securitization activities, and other contingent liquidity risks that were not well managed during the financial market turmoil;*
> - *Aligning the risk-taking incentives of individual business units with the liquidity risk exposures their activities create for the bank;*
> - *Stress tests that cover a variety of institution-specific and market-wide scenarios, with a link to the development of effective contingency funding plans;*
> - *Strong management of intraday liquidity risks and collateral positions;*
> - *Maintenance of a robust cushion of unencumbered, high-quality, liquid assets to be in a position to survive protracted periods of liquidity stress; and*
> - *Regular public disclosures, both quantitative and qualitative, of a bank's liquidity risk profile and management.*

> *The principles also strengthen expectations about the role of supervisors, including the need to intervene in a timely manner to address deficiencies and the importance of communication with other supervisors and public authorities, both within and across national borders."*

---

13   http://www.bis.org/publ/bcbs144.pdf

Many of these issues have been addressed in prior sections, so we will touch only on the unique points.

Firm-wide Liquidity Risk Tolerance
By setting a policy in advance and at the aggregate level, bank managers design a target maximum exposure to liquidity demands. Once the aggregate maximum is set and the calculations of liquidity risk are completed, banks can determine if corrective action is required.

Align Risk-Taking Incentives
A risk-taking department that has free rein to take liquidity risk will certainly squander it. To ensure that the bank's capacity for taking liquidity risk is not compromised by a single department, the bank must place a cost on the risk, i.e., penalize the business for taking excessive liquidity risk, and measure the performance of the business after computing the cost of its liquidity risk positions.

Stress Tests
While market-risk tests of liquidity are fairly commonplace, it is necessary for banks to also run their stress tests on liquidity scenarios. These stress tests combine market events (e.g., falling interest rates) with credit events (increasing defaults) and bank-specific events (a declining credit rating that triggers collateral calls). The stress tests must be designed to capture a wide range of realistic, unlikely yet possible outcomes.

Regular Public Reporting and Disclosures
It is in the bank's interest to inform its stakeholders how well liquidity is managed. Customers, debtholders, and equityholders all prefer that a bank does not get into financial distress, and the leading cause of bank distress is liquidity risk.

3.4 Funds Transfer Pricing

Funds Transfer Pricing (FTP) is a modern name for a process that has been fundamental to ALM since the origins of banking. It refers to the charging and paying of interest from a central location within the bank, typically the Treasury. It assures that funding is available for asset gathering business lines at a reasonable and known cost, while simultaneously assuring that liability gathering business lines can off-load the liquidity they have gathered at a reasonable and known level of income.

The two traditional business models in banking—commercial banking and investment banking—have fundamentally different approaches to funding the asset gathering businesses they manage. Commercial banks base their lending on deposits taken at their own branches, while investment banks fund themselves in the interbank and/or capital markets. As retail depositors are known to be "sticky"—not likely to withdraw deposits even if a bank is in trouble—it is relatively safe for commercial banks to fund loans. Investment banks, on the other hand, rely mostly on professional, wholesale markets for funding. This funding source is often less costly and available in larger volume, but at the same time it is brittle. It has little "staying power," meaning if a bank gets into trouble the professional funding sources tend to dry up very fast. Both Northern Rock[14] (2007) in the UK and Bear Stearns[15] (2008) in the US provide examples of what happens to banks when the wholesale markets have dried up for them.

FTP is at the center of ALM, as it centralizes interest rate exposures from all business areas within a bank. As such it helps to establish a margin over cost of funds to the liability gathering activities, as well as a margin to be charged from the asset gathering activities of the bank.

There are several additional benefits from operating a centralized FTP operation:

1. By transferring interest rate risk to a central location, business lines' balance sheets are rendered immune from interest rate risk
2. By charging for funds transfers, FTP helps determine the Net Interest Income (NII) for each business unit
3. By virtue of its position in the supply chain for funding, FTP is effectively a tool for managing a bank's liquidity risk

Figure 3.7 is a simplification of Treasury's central role in the flow of funds through the bank. The five-year loan is match funded, leaving no interest rate or liquidity risk. While seemingly an ideal situation, when taken beyond a single loan and a single liability, this process gives liability gatherers a significant degree of granularity to overcome. It would not be practical or feasible to match each of a bank's millions of individual loans with specific liabilities. Furthermore, Treasury would not be able to capture incremental profits by funding at different maturities that might be less expensive. In this Figure the net Interest margin (NIM) contribution by Treasury is nil.

---

14   https://en.wikipedia.org/wiki/Northern_Rock
15   https://en.wikipedia.org/wiki/Bear_Stearns

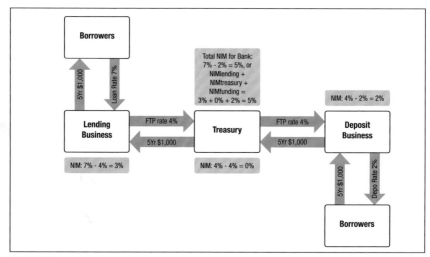

FIGURE 3.7 FTP – No Interest Rate or Liquidity Risk – Treasury Pass-through

Figure 3.8 evolves from Figure 3.7. Note that the deposit rate is now 1%, which goes with a shorter liability maturity of two years. Under this model, the Treasury is now contributing net interest margin, in addition to the NIM from lending and deposit-taking, respectively. The overall NIM of the bank has increased.

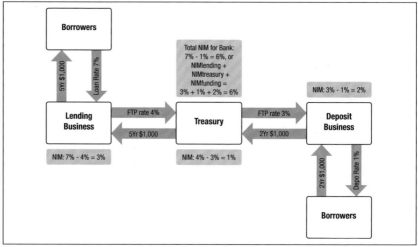

FIGURE 3.8 FTP – Interest Rate and Liquidity Management Centralized – Treasury Maturity Transformation

There are four approaches, or methods, that Treasury can take to optimize NIM, while simultaneously minimizing liquidity risk for the bank:

1. Cost of Funds Method
2. Net Funding Method
3. Pooled Funding Method
4. Matched Maturity Method

3.4.1 Cost of Funds Method

Under this method Treasury calculates the weighted average rate of funds raised and uses this rate to provide funds to all business units.

Knowing their target cost of funds, business units decide which assets to acquire. This could have unintended effects, in particular a bias towards high-yield lending opportunities when funding costs are on the rise. Over the long run this could increase the overall credit risk in the balance sheet. Also, the interest rollover cycles determined by Treasury may not be attractive to either borrowers or depositors.

3.4.2 Net Funding Method

Under this method, business units raise their own funds as needed and only turn to central Treasury to borrow additional net funds or to park or invest surplus net funds.

This method leads to significant duplication of effort. In a modern bank there would likely have to be a funding department for each of the retail, commercial, corporate, and investment banking divisions. Retail might need a separate funding department for its credit card business. And a central Treasury function would still be needed to provide net top-up funding to, or take surplus liquidity from, each business unit.

Maturity mismatches would be rife. Few business units would be able to self-fund at the maturities required by the loan customers, leading to significant problems estimating interest rate and liquidity risk in the whole Bank.

3.4.3 Pooled Funding Method

Business units need to be segregated into asset-focused and liability-focused divisions to make practical use of this method. Treasury provides separate FTP rates for lending and deposits based on market rates and own cost of funds. IT systems need to be robust in order to be able to disseminate accurate market-based rates to all business units without delay.

Under this model, Treasury earns a spread between the two FTP rates and in the process becomes a net contributor to a bank's profitability. It is not advisable, however, to allow Treasury the full scope to maximize profits or to play to its own self-interest. A more conservative approach would look at Treasury's income contribution as a way of quantifying and managing the bank's overall NII.

3.4.4 Matched Maturity Method

Under this model, Treasury is not only a central utility, but a vital market place pricing costs of funds and deposit returns separately and transparently to the whole bank. Treasury develops optimal transfer pricing curves, which effectively must match external market yield curves to avoid building arbitrage risk into the bank's business activities. That is, it must avoid pricing instruments at a level that would allow external counterparties to buy an instrument from one business unit and sell a linked instrument back to another business unit for an overall profit to the external counterparty and loss to the bank.

3.5 Risk Reporting

Based on its experience with banks during the credit crisis, the Federal Deposit Insurance Corporation (FDIC), one of the main US banking regulators, has suggested[16] that banks should also create risk reports that address the following potential risk areas. These reports should be produced in addition to the usual probabilistic analysis and stress tests.

- Cash flow gaps
- Asset and funding concentration
- Critical assumptions used in credit projections
- Key early warning or risk indicators
- Funding availability
- Status of contingent funding sources
- Collateral uses

---

16   Financial Institution Letter FIL-84-2008,
https://www.fdic.gov/news/news/financial/2008/fil08084.html

JPMorgan Chase discussed liquidity risk management extensively in its 2013 Annual Report (pp. 168-173). The major headings include governance, funding, and credit ratings.

Governance
JPM's liquidity risk management is centralized in the treasury function. The ALCO (asset-liability committee) is responsible for the execution of the liquidity policy and the contingency funding plan. In sum, the group's responsibility is to measure, monitor, report, and manage liquidity risk. The Annual Report says:

In the context of the Firm's liquidity management, Treasury is responsible for:

- Measuring, managing, monitoring, and reporting the Firm's current and projected liquidity sources and uses;
- Understanding the liquidity characteristics of the Firm's assets and liabilities;
- Defining and monitoring firmwide and legal-entity liquidity strategies, policies, guidelines, and contingency funding plans;
- Liquidity stress testing under a variety of adverse scenarios;
- Managing funding mix and deployment of excess short-term cash;
- Defining and implementing funds transfer pricing ("FTP") across all lines of business and regions; and
- Defining and addressing the impact of regulatory changes on funding and liquidity.

The Firm has a liquidity risk governance framework to review, approve, and monitor the implementation of liquidity risk policies at the firmwide, regional, and line of business levels.

Funding
The Annual Report says:

> "*The Firm funds its global balance sheet through diverse sources of funding including a stable deposit franchise as well as secured and unsecured funding in the capital markets.*"

Sources of funds include the stable portion of deposits, the stable portion of liability balances, and a variety of short- and long-term instruments. The latter category includes purchased federal funds, commercial paper, bank notes, long-term debt and trust-preferred capital debt securities.

Flexibility in funding is afforded by JPMorgan Chase's reserves of unencumbered and liquid securities. These securities can be loaned in the repo market or sold in the asset securitization markets.

Credit Ratings

Credit rating changes can have an enormous impact on liquidity, but for JPMorgan Chase in 2013, the sensitivity to ratings changes was relatively low.

The Annual Report says:

> *"The cost and availability of financing are influenced by credit ratings. Reductions in these ratings could have an adverse effect on the Firm's access to liquidity sources, increase the cost of funds, trigger additional collateral or funding requirements, and decrease the number of investors and counterparties willing to lend to the Firm."*

3.6 Basel III Liquidity Measures

The extremely difficult liquidity situation in international banking markets during 2008 was as much the cause of the credit crisis as it was a result of it. The preceding decade had been characterized by freely—or almost freely—available credit: availability was only a function of price. As long as a bank was willing to pay the asking price for liquidity it was made available. This situation was even heralded by bankers as the arrival of true market-based banking. If an asset was deemed to be risky, it would be funded at a high spread. It was assumed that the propensity for taking on risky assets would be self-regulating, so the higher the cost of funds, the less demand for funds and, in turn, fewer risky assets would be in demand. This turned out not to be true.

In 2008 the Basel Committee on Banking Supervision (BCBS) published a document entitled, "Principles for Sound Liquidity Risk Management and Supervision"[17] as the foundation of its bank liquidity management framework.

The BCBS subsequently publicized a white paper at the end of 2009[18] explaining market best practice for liquidity management in banks and

---

17   http://www.bis.org/publ/bcbs144.pdf
18   BCBS International Framework for Liquidity Risk Measurement, Standards and Monitoring: (2009-12) http://www.bis.org/publ/bcbs165.pdf

followed up a year later by confirming two specific measures for liquidity risk management in the Basel III proposal of 2010.[19]

The two measures are the Liquidity Coverage Ratio (LCR),[20] a short-term liquidity measure, and the Net Stable Funding Ratio (NSFR), a longer-term measure. The objective of both measures is to ensure a bank's survivability, should it come under funding pressure, in the short and long term. It is important to keep in mind that, due to the nature of the Bank for International Settlements, of which the BCBS is part, the two measures look at survivability in the face of external, systemic causes, such as market-wide shocks. The measures do not address liquidity management from an institution's internal point of view. That element is still left to banks to deal with themselves.

3.6.1 Liquidity Coverage Ratio

The formula for the Basel III LCR is straightforward:

$$LCR: \frac{Stock\ of\ high\ quality\ assets}{Total\ net\ cash\ outflows\ over\ the\ next\ 30\ calendar\ days} \geq 100\%$$

High quality liquid assets (HQLA) are further defined below, as are net cash outflows (NCO). Key to understanding this ratio is that in a stress scenario, whatever the bank has "stocked up" must be used and must be sufficient over the first 30 days of a liquidity crisis.

However, the LCR is a complex ratio, as is clear from the fact that the BCBS document that explains its details runs to 75 pages. (Basel III: The Liquidity Coverage Ratio and liquidity risk monitoring tools (Jan 2013), http://www.bis.org/publ/bcbs238.pdf.)

Before delving into the technical details of the formula, it makes sense to ask whether a liquidity crisis has ever lasted fewer than 30 days. The answer is that most liquidity crises last for longer than that. Systemic liquidity crises can drag on for many years, but the LCR does not take account of such long, drawn out crises.

If a single bank makes a miscalculation and finds itself unable to fund itself overnight there may be marketwide impacts for a short period of time if the bank is large enough, but it is unlikely that the problem would last as long as a month.

During this month, the rest of the banking system would have to function without a significant player and that could easily cause liquidity

---

19   BCBS (2010-12) http://www.bis.org/publ/bcbs188.pdf
20   BCBS (2013-01) http://www.bis.org/publ/bcbs238.pdf

stress. As a result, some people see the LCR simply as a measure to address the risk of minor problems that have little systemic significance (a bit like a "band aid" that is used on minor cuts and bruises).

Net Cash Outflows
Total net cash outflows are defined as follows:

> *Total net cash outflows over the next 30 calendar days =*
> *Total expected cash outflows*
> *– Min{total expected cash inflows; 75% of total expected cash outflows}*

The NCO formula is tricky because the 75% minimum limiter is on outgoing cash, not incoming cash. In other words, for a bank with good/ strong cash inflow over the next 30 days, 75% of the outflow may be the smaller amount, in which case NCO is fixed at 25% of cash flow.

As an example, assume a bank has 100 (in USD) cash inflow and 100 outflow. In this case the NCO is 25 (25% of the cash outflows). The same is true for a bank with USD 200 cash inflow and 100 outflow: NCO is 25 (25% of the cash outflow). And even for a bank with 75 cash inflow and 100 cash outflow, NCO is still 25. There is only a difference if cash inflows are below 75% of outflows, i.e., a bank with 65 cash inflow and 100 cash outflow will have a NCO of 35.

The interpretation of the ratio above is that a bank must maintain a stock of highly liquid assets equal to or larger than 25% of its cash outflows over the next 30 days.

HQLA
HQLAs are described in a long list of assets that, from a regulatory standpoint, are deemed to be sufficiently liquid, even during times of stress. The list is divided, in order of liquidity quality, into Level 1, Level 2A, and Level 2B assets. Assets must be unencumbered.

Level 1 Assets
This level comprises the highest possible asset quality and includes: cash, central bank reserves, marketable securities issued by sovereigns, central banks, Public Sector Entities (PSEs), the BIS itself, the IMF, the European Central Bank, the European Community, and multilateral development banks, such as the World Bank. They must be assigned a 0% RWA weighting under the Basel II Standardized Approach, meaning they must be minimum AA rated. No haircuts are applied to Level 1 assets.

Level 2A Assets
This level comprises securities representing claims on or guaranteed by sovereigns, central banks, PSEs, or multilateral development banks, that have been assigned a 20% RWA weighting under Basel II Standardized Approach. This maps to a rating of A+ to A–.

It also comprises corporate debt, commercial paper and covered bonds that are not issued by a financial institution. They must hold a rating of AA– or higher.

Level 2B Assets
This level includes Residential Mortgage-Backed Securities (after applying a 75% haircut), with a maximum Loan-To-Value ratio of 80% and a rating AA or higher. It also includes corporate bonds rated between A– and BBB–, and exchange traded stocks in non-financial issuers that are also constituents in a major domestic equity index (subject to a 50% haircut).

Level 2B assets may not account for more than 15% of the total stock of HQLAs, while Level 2A and 2B assets combined may not account for more than 40% of the total stock of HQLAs.

The formula for calculating HQLAs is:

$$Stock\ of\ HQLA =$$
$$Level\ 1 + Level\ 2A + Level\ 2B - Max(((Adjusted\ Level\ 2A +$$
$$Adjusted\ Level\ 2B) - 2/3 \times Adjusted\ Level\ 1), (Adjusted\ Level\ 2B - 15/85$$
$$\times (Adjusted\ Level\ 1 + Adjusted\ Level\ 2A), 0)).$$

This is quite a convoluted formula, but essentially HQLAs consist of the sum of Level 1, 2A, and 2B assets minus the maximum of three possible variables:

1. L2A + L2B – (2/3 of L1);
2. L2B – (17.65% of L1+L2A); or
3. Zero.

Zero would be nice in the context of the LCR, but is generally only possible when Level 1 assets are larger than 2A and several orders of magnitude larger than 2B assets.

If a bank holds only Level 1 HQLAs and neither 2A nor 2B assets, then the full amount of Level 1 assets count towards the ratio. However, Level 2A and 2B assets are subject to restrictive caps and adjustments, so that, as a bank holds more of them, the overall HQLAs are reduced.

Consider this example: a bank holds 150 Adjusted Level 1, 43 Adjusted Level 2A, and 17 Adjusted Level 2B assets. Using the formula, the result is:

$$150 + 43 + 17 - Max\{[(43 + 17) - (2/3 \times 150)],$$
$$[17 - ((15/85) \times (150+43))], 0\}.$$

This becomes

$$150 + 43 + 17 - Max(-40, -17, 0), \text{ or}$$
$$150 + 43 + 17 - 0 = 210.$$

This is effectively the maximum allowed net cash outflow for a bank for the next 30 days. This is not too bad, since all assets count in this case. L2A and L2B assets could be higher, but only 40% of the sum is eligible in the calculation.

But, try to invert the assets: if L1 = 17, L2A = 43 and L2B = 150, the calculation looks like this:

$$17 + 43 + 150 - Max\{[(43 +150) - (2/3 \times 17)],$$
$$[150 - ((15/85) \times (17 + 43))], 0\}, \text{ or}$$

$$17 + 43 + 150 - Max(181.67, 139.41, 0), \text{ or}$$

$$17 + 43 + 150 - 181.66 = 28.34.$$

This is only marginally higher than the total L1 assets and a frighteningly small value for a Treasury risk manager. Indeed, if this bank has 100 (in USD) cash inflow and 100 cash outflow over the next 30 days, the HQLA's are just barely enough to allow the bank to continue operating, with a ratio of $(28.34/(100 - 75\% \times 100)) = 113.36\%$. Just 13.36% more cash outflows than inflows and the ratio goes down to 100%!

Any breaches, even expected future breaches, to this rule must be reported immediately to regulators.

The LCR came into force on January 1, 2015. Banks are, however, only required to apply 60% of the ratio for the first year, rising by 10% per year until reaching the full amount (100%) in 2019.

A final point to bear in mind is that all of the calculations given above must be repeated for each of the currencies, defined as 5% or more, the bank actively funds itself in.

3.6.2 Net Stable Funding Ratio

The NSFR is presented as a long-term measure for bank liquidity and is intended to discourage overreliance on short-term, wholesale-based funding at banks. Given the one-year time horizon of the NSFR it is probably just a medium-term measure. The NFSR is supposed to guide banks to fund themselves from sources that are sufficiently stable to mitigate the risk of future funding stress.

The NSFR ratio is defined as follows:

$$\frac{Available\ amount\ of\ Stable\ Funding\ (ASF)}{Required\ amount\ of\ Stable\ Funding\ (RSF)} \geq 100\%$$

The available amount of stable funding is defined according to Figure 3.9, where liabilities are multiplied by an ASF factor before being applied:

Type of liability	ASF factor
Tier 1 plus Tier 2 capital	100%
Preferred stock not included in Tier 2 with effective maturity of one year or greater taking into account any explicit or embedded options that would reduce the expected maturity to less than one year	100%
Secured and unsecured funding with effective maturities of one year or greater, excluding any instruments with explicit or embedded options that would reduce the expected maturity to less than one year	90%
Stable (as defined in the LCR) retail/small business non-maturity deposits and/or term deposits with residual maturities of less than one year	80%
Less stable (as defined in the LCR) retail/small business non-maturity deposits and/or term deposits with less than one-year residual maturity	50%
Unsecured wholesale funding, non-maturity deposits and/or term deposits with residual maturity less than one year provided by non-financial customers, sovereigns, central banks, multilateral development banks, and PSEs	0%
All other liabilities and equity not included above	0%

FIGURE 3.9: ASF Liabilities

The required amount of stable funding is defined according to Figure 3.10, where assets are multiplied by a RSF factor before being applied:

Type of exposure	RSF factor
Cash, short-term unsecured instruments, securities with less than one-year residual maturity and with no embedded option that would extend maturity to more than one year, securities with exactly offsetting reverse repurchase transactions, less than one-year unencumbered loans to financial entities	0%
Unencumbered longer-dated sovereign/public sector securities having 0% risk weight under the Basel II standardized approach and with active repo markets	5%
Unencumbered AA-rated or higher longer-dated corporate bonds that meet all conditions for Level 2 assets in the LCR; unencumbered longer-dated sovereign/public sector securities with 20% risk weight under the Basel II standardized approach, which meet all the conditions for Level 2 assets in LCR	20%
Unencumbered gold, equities traded on a major exchange and not issued by financial institutions, non-financial corporate or covered bonds rated A+ to A-, central bank eligible and traded in a deep and active market with low concentration	50%
Less than one-year residual maturity unencumbered loans to non-financial corporate clients, sovereigns, central banks and PSEs	50%
Unencumbered residential mortgages and other loans qualifying for 35% or lower risk weight under Basel II standardized approach	65%
Less than one-year residual maturity unencumbered loans to retail clients and small business customers other than those qualifying for the 65% RSF	85%
All other assets	100%

FIGURE 3.10 RSF assets

Banks must seek to maximize the ASF liabilities, while simultaneously minimizing RSF assets. ASF is maximized by emphasis on core equity, preferred stock, secured funding, and retail deposits. RSF is minimized by emphasis on cash, sovereign and PSE securities, corporate securities rated AA or higher, and non-financial stocks trading on major exchanges.

Keep in mind that there are separate, additional ASF/RSF lists for derivatives positions. The student is encouraged to refer to the BCBS document for further detail. (Basel III: the net stable funding ratio (2014-10), http://www.bis.org/bcbs/publ/d295.pdf)

Although the lists above are relatively self-explanatory, Figure 3.11 below illustrates just how difficult it is for banks to comply. Any NSFR below 100% is non-compliant.

Large European Banks' Reported Net Stable Funding Ratio at end 2013	
	%
ABN AMRO Bank NV	105
Barclays Bank PLC	110
Rabobank Nederland NV	114
Credit Suisse NG	>100
Erste Group Bank AG	>100[a]
KBC Group NV	111
Royal Bank of Scotland PLC	122
Standard Chartered Bank	110–120
Swedbank AB	97
UBS AG	109

[a] As at the third quarter 2013   *Source:* Standard and Poor's

FIGURE 3.11 NSFR of Large European Banks, Year End 2013[21]

3.6.3 Liquidity Reporting Standards

Regulatory reporting should be conducted on a monthly basis for the LCR ratio and on a quarterly basis for the NSFR ratio according to the Basel standards. However, the LCR reporting frequency could be weekly, or even daily, at the discretion of national regulatory supervisors. This would typically happen during times of liquidity stress.

Disclosure templates for both LCR and NSFR ratios are provided below.

Basel standards require reporting on a group basis for those banks that are designated as "Strategically Important Financial Institutions" (SIFIs), and national supervisors may also request reporting from subsets of entities of SIFI's, or even from non-SIFI banks.

---

21   Excerpt from speech by BCBS Chairman Stefan Ingves, May 15, 2014.

(In local currency)	TOTAL UNWEIGHTED[a] VALUE (average)	TOTAL WEIGHTED[b] VALUE (average)
HIGH-QUALITY LIQUID ASSETS		
1 Total high-quality liquid assets (HQLA)		
CASH OUTFLOWS		
2 Retail deposits and deposits from small business customers of which		
3 *Stable deposits*		
4 *Less stable deposits*		
5 Unsecured wholesale funding, of which		
6 *Operational deposits (all counterparties) and deposits in networks of cooperative banks*		
7 *Non-operational deposits (all counterparties)*		
8 *Unsecured debt*		
9 Secured wholesale funding		
10 Additional requirements, of which		
11 *Outflows related to derivative exposures and other collateral requirements*		
12 *Outflows related to loss of funding on debt products*		
13 *Credit and liquidity facilities*		
14 Other contractual funding obligations		
15 Other contingent funding obligations		
16 TOTAL CASH OUTFLOWS		
CASH INFLOWS		
17 Secured lending (e.g. reverse repos)		
18 Inflows from fully performing exposures		
19 Other cash inflows		
20 TOTAL CASH INFLOWS		
		TOTAL ADJUSTED[c] VALUE
21 TOTAL HQLA		
22 TOTAL NET CASH OUTFLOWS		
23 LIQUIDITY COVERAGE RATIO (%)		

FIGURE 3.12   LCR common disclosure template

(in currency amount)	Unweighted value				Weighted value
	No maturity	< 6 months	6 months to < 1 yr	≥ 1 yr	
ASF Item					
1	Capital:				
2	Regulatory capital				
3	Other capital instruments				
4	Retail deposits and deposits from small business customers:				
5	Stable deposits				
6	Less stable deposits				
7	Wholesale funding:				
8	Operational deposits				
9	Other wholesale funding				
10	Liabilities with matching interdependent assets				
11	Other liabilities				
12	Net derivative liabilities				
13	All other liabilities and equity not included in the above categories				
14	**Total ASF**				
RSF Item					
15	Total high-quality liquid assets (HQLA)				
16	Deposits held at other financial institutions for operational purposes				
17	Performing loans and securities				
18	Performing loans to financial institutions secured by Level 1 HQLA				
19	Performing loans to financial institutions secured by non-Level 1 HQLA and unsecured performing loans to financial institutions				
20	Performing loans to non-financial corporate clients, loans to retail and small business customers, and loans to sovereigns, central banks and PSEs, of which:				
21	With a risk weight of less than or equal to 35% under the Basel II Standardised Approach for credit risk				
22	Performing residential mortgages, of which:				
23	With a risk weight of less than or equal to 35% under the Basel II Standardised Approach for credit risk				
24	Securities that are not in default and do not qualify as HQLA, including exchange-traded equities				

25	Assets with matching interdependent liabilities					
26	Other assets:					
27	*Physical traded commodities, including gold*					
28	*Net derivative assets*					
29	*All other assets not included in the above categories*					
30	Off-balance sheet items					
31	**Total RSF**					
32	**Net Stable Funding Ratio (%)**					

FIGURE 3.13   NSFR common disclosure template

3.7 Conclusions

Liquidity risk management during normal times can be as simple as cash management. In periods of high volatility and uncertain credit conditions, liquidity issues become paramount, as they threaten a bank's health and even its existence. Whereas banks use liquidity ladders to understand their static liquidity position, probabilistic models are needed to understand the behavior of complex assets and liabilities, and their effect on a bank's liquidity. Also, stress testing can be done on these models to determine a bank's maximum likely liquidity requirement.

Liquidity can be supplied by the bank itself (selling assets), by the strength of the bank's balance sheet (borrowings), or by external parties. The bank's liquidity position, both sources and uses of cash, is usually managed as part of the asset and liability management function of the bank.

3.8 Summary

This chapter addressed risks associated with liquidity, and how to identify, measure and manage them.

Introduction to Liquidity Risk
- Interest rate risk in the banking book is the risk of loss due to adverse changes in interest rates.
- Liquidity risk in the banking book is the risk of not being able to fund the holding of an asset or the retirement of a liability.
- Liquidity risk management is a vital area of risk control.
- Historically, liquidity management was focused on by estimating depositor behavior and drawdowns on credit lines.

- Currently, liquidity problems can arise due to leveraged lending (if asset values fall), margin requirements, and counterparty defaults.
- Banks address their needs with their endogenous, exogenous, and external liquidity.
- Endogenous liquidity is the liquidity inherent in bank assets themselves.
- Exogenous liquidity (often called funding liquidity) is the liquidity provided to the bank by its liability structure, including its ability to borrow and obtain contingent lines.
- External liquidity is the noncontractual contingent capital supplied by investors and other institutions to support a bank during times of liquidity stress.
- Liquidity mismatches can cause serious problems, as was highlighted by the crisis at Long-Term Capital Management (LTCM), a US hedge fund.
- As a direct result of the LTCM crisis, many trading businesses now ensure that they have better access to long-term funding through instruments such as committed funding lines (i.e., commercial bank commitments to lend to them).

Liquidity Risk Measurement
- The classic tool for measuring the bank's liquidity position is the liquidity ladder, a snapshot of the bank's projected cash flow sources and uses.
- The liquidity ladder is usually produced to assess short-term liquidity requirements.
- Gaps in liquidity can be filled by selling assets, drawing down credit lines, or issuing securities.
- The biggest problem with the liquidity ladder approach is that it does not address the probabilistic nature of cash flow requirements.
- No one can predict with certainty runs on the bank or customer demands for cash on their credit lines.
- As a result, the best models consider the range of possible outcomes for liquidity demand, and the drivers of those outcomes.
- Liquidity models have the same level of complexity as VaR models and credit models, and the same shortfalls, such as reliance on past relationships and problems integrating risks across related assets.

Liquidity Risk Management
- Under normal circumstances, liquidity risk is well-behaved and relatively easy to manage.
- During times of stress, banks turn to security issuance, interbank or government loans, obtaining additional credit lines, and selling or securitizing assets.
- As an example of security issuance, during the global financial crisis, Goldman Sachs issued USD 5 billion in preferred stocks to Warren Buffett in order to help the company improve its liquidity position.
- Securitization of bank assets is the process by which banks issue bonds where the payment of interest and repayment of principal on the bonds depends on the cash flow generated by a "pool" of bank assets, and the bank has transferred its legal rights to payment of interest and repayment of principal to the bondholders.
- When banks create such bond issues they greatly increase the inherent (endogenous) liquidity of the assets that have been securitized.
- In the US it is common for banks to securitize many of their retail assets on a continuous basis and then hold the assets in securitized form.

Risk Reporting
- At a minimum, banks should prepare liquidity ladders, probabilistic analysis, and stress tests of their liquidity requirements.
- In addition, in the US the FDIC recommends reports related to cash flow gaps, asset and funding concentration, critical assumptions used in credit projections, key early warning or risk indicators, funding availability, status of contingent funding sources, and collateral uses.
- Excerpts of JPMorgan Chase's 2013 liquidity risk reporting are provided in the chapter.

CHAPTER 4

Bank Capital Management

This chapter explains how the concepts of risk studied in the earlier chapters drive capital management decisions for banks. For banks, risk is a better measure of required capital than capital itself; models that estimate risk form the foundation for assessments of capital adequacy both for individual banks and the entire financial system.

This chapter reviews, sharpens, and builds on prior descriptions of capital and its components: the different types of capital, and how capital is computed, managed, and increased or decreased.

A bank does not calculate capital solely in order to satisfy its regulators. The ultimate purpose of understanding capital is to optimize risk-adjusted return on capital (RAROC) for different activities and make financial decisions that maximize bank shareholder value relative to risk taken.

While every student of banking should understand regulatory capital, the focus of this volume has been on the economics of risk management and not on the regulation of risk management. However, because regulatory capital restricts the actions of banks, it is critical to consider it from an economic perspective as well.

On completion of this chapter the reader will have an improved understanding of:

- The types of capital
- Regulatory and economic capital

- The components of Tier 1, Tier 2, and Tier 3 capital
- Capital deductions
- The ratios between different capital components
- The capital creation process
- The relationship between capital and risk measures
- Return and risk for economic capital (RAROC)
- Risk-based performance measurement at the bank level
- The importance of a culture of risk management

The final point may be the most important. If risk is the measure of capital for a bank, then bank managers must strive to maximize risk awareness and develop consistent standards for taking and avoiding risk. A common language—for risks, measures of risk, and return on risk—facilitates the development of the risk management culture.

4.1 Types Of Capital

The management of a bank differs from the management of non-financial corporations. One important difference is that banks, unrestrained, might have incentives to increase their risks as much as possible. Suppose for example that a bank had USD 100 million in capital but borrowed USD 100 billion to lend. If very few loans defaulted, the bank could profit enormously. Conversely, if there were larger than expected defaults, the bank would not lose more than USD 100 million. Without regulation, there would be incentive to take excess risk. Even though depositors might be protected by deposit insurance agencies, the financial system would not be protected against excessive risk-taking by financial institutions collectively.

As another example of the difference between banks and non-financial corporations, consider the objectives of the two different corporation types. While a non-financial corporation may strive to maximize return on capital, a banker may not even know exactly how to measure capital. For example, if the bank enters into a number of futures trades, how should it compute the capital needed to support such trades, particularly if no cash is put on margin to guarantee the trades or if the margin is in the form of interest-bearing securities?

As a third example, consider a bank that has issued debt. Debt puts cash into the bank, but at the same time, repayment provisions can jeopardize the sufficiency of the capital base. Should the debt be counted as part of the capital of the bank? Or, should it be given partial capital treatment to recognize the capital contribution on the one hand, but the obligation to repay on the other? The answer is not obvious.

Because international governments have an interest in preserving the integrity of the international banking system, they have passed regulations requiring minimum capital levels at banks. This requires that they define capital requirements reasonably, determine how capital is measured, and determine the appropriate forms of eligible capital for banks. Too much capital means banks can be inefficient and uncompetitive. Too little capital jeopardizes the health of the financial system.

4.1.1 Economic and Regulatory Capital

In non-financial firms, capital is the amount of funds and assets required to establish and run a business. Typically, capital is equity capital—the investment made by the owners in the firm as paid-in capital—which can be made through a cash infusion or a security issuance. Long-term borrowings can also be considered as capital, but not as equity capital. While companies generally try to maximize their return on invested capital, they usually take capital to be equal to the total amount of paid-in capital, or at least the amount of paid-in equity. Banks, however, due to significantly higher leverage, may lose much more than the paid-in capital; their possible losses may exceed the amount of capital contributed from all their capital sources. Their possible losses, their capital at risk, or the level of losses the bank feels comfortable with, i.e., their risk capital, may exceed paid-in capital. This is exactly what regulators hope to avoid, since unexpected loss events could cause the failure of not just one bank, but many banks simultaneously.

If banks were unregulated, their decisions on how much capital to hold would probably be driven primarily by a desire to optimize their return on capital and would be based on their own internal calculations. This type of capital calculation is known as economic capital (also risk capital), since it reflects the economic tradeoffs of the bank as accurately as the bank can represent them. The capital measures defined by regulators are known as regulatory capital. As a general rule, economic capital is determined by internal risk models, whereas regulatory capital is determined by rules imposed by an external authority.

Advantages of Economic Capital
Economic capital is generally believed to be a better measure of capital for a bank than regulatory capital, because economic capital reflects the possible losses the bank can bear based on the bank's own estimates of the risks it is

taking. In contrast, regulatory capital reflects the lowest level of capital the bank may have to meet the regulatory requirement. Arguably, banks are in a better position to understand their risks, and are motivated to understand them better than anyone else, so regulators expect bankers to have a more subtle and complete understanding of their capital. Since banks are putting their money at risk based on the capital calculations, they will do their best to ensure the calculations are accurate at the appropriate level of commercial standard.

The global financial crisis of 2007-2009 highlighted clear differences of opinion on this point, with many arguments against bankers on account of their putting other people's money at risk, not their own. Many countries changed bankers' compensation from cash to equity, with long vesting periods and clawback provisions, designed to keep bankers' interests in line with shareholders' and civil society's. It is an open question, however, whether these measures will have any measurable impact in the long run.

Disadvantages of Economic Capital
Since the models for economic capital are derived by the banks themselves, regulators may be concerned that the models may be insufficient, unused, subject to significant model risk, or even manipulated. For these reasons, regulators would not likely accept capital constraints for banks linked purely to internal economic capital models.

Benefits of Regulatory Capital
From a regulatory perspective, internal models of economic capital are problematic as every bank uses a different model. If banks use different models, it is difficult for a regulator to determine which banks are well capitalized or poorly capitalized relative to their business activities. For this reason, regulatory standards impose formulaic capital calculations for all of a bank's activities. In addition to the benefit of capital comparability across banks, regulatory calculations can help ensure that (a) banks are not missing key risks in their models and (b) banks are not using the capital calculations in any obvious way to "game" the banking regulation system.

Disadvantages of Regulatory Capital
By requiring formulaic interpretations of capital, regulatory models tend to overstate economic risk. For example, in early regulatory frameworks, all corporate debt was deemed to have the same risk level. While this helped regulators quickly compare risks across banks, it caused banks to shift to riskier corporate debts, because the returns were higher and the regulatory

capital was the same. These types of activities became known as regulatory capital arbitrage.

4.1.2 Balancing Economic and Regulatory Capital

Which capital measure should a bank use for its internal decisions? If a bank has confidence in its economic capital model, it will use that model for decisions, but recognize that it has constraints on regulatory capital. This implies that while regulatory capital is an important guide for banks, it does not govern how they allocate their capital, except in cases where the regulatory capital calculations are much higher than economic capital. In these cases, it may be more important to focus on regulatory capital as a guide to making decisions.

When looking at regulatory capital limits as a constraint on economic capital allocation, a bank's objective is to maximize its return on economic capital, after adjusting for the cost of regulatory capital constraints. The most popular measure of economic capital is RAROC, the risk-adjusted return on capital, which is discussed at length later in this chapter. For now, we focus on the components of capital and the key issues of regulatory capital so the student can best understand the relationships between them.

4.1.3 JPMorgan Chase's Economic Risk Capital

JPMorgan Chase measures economic risk capital using internal risk-assessment methodologies and models based primarily on four risk factors: credit, market, operational, and private equity risk, considering factors, assumptions, and inputs that differ from those required to be used for regulatory capital requirements. Accordingly economic risk capital provides a complementary measure to regulatory capital.

In years prior to 2013, JPMorgan Chase reported balance sheet amounts for Total Common Stockholders' Equity as the sum of Economic Capital, Goodwill, and Other, which covered additional capital required for the bank to comply with minimum capital rules. While Goodwill was USD 48 billion in 2013, there is no value given for the incremental capital labeled Other.

Due to the uncertainties regarding the final Basel III wording for Economic Capital values, and "as economic risk capital is a separate component of the capital framework for Advanced Approach banking organizations under Basel III, the Firm is currently in the process of enhancing its economic risk capital framework to address the Basel III interim final rule."[22]

---

22   JPMorgan Chase, 2013 Annual Report

4.2 Computing Economic Capital

Economic capital is a measure of a bank's capital requirement that relates directly to the aggregate risk the bank is running, in effect its ability to meet unexpected losses in excess of expected losses. To survive in the long term a bank needs to overcome periods during which extreme circumstances could cause it to sustain large losses. If the bank has capital levels to support it through such times it will survive; if it does not, it will fail.

4.2.1 Economic Capital and Value-at-risk (VaR)

The use of economic capital as a measure of risk stems directly from the development of Value-at-risk (VaR) methodology which took place in the trading businesses of banks. The VaR methodology provided a successful tool for both supervisors and bank management.

A bank's risk report may typically contain a statement similar to: "The trading portfolio has a daily VaR of USD 5 million at the 99% confidence level." In this statement the confidence level relates to a level of probability that some event will occur. In simple terms, the VaR expressed above says that within the period of one trading day there is a 1% (100%-99%) chance that losses on the trading portfolio could exceed USD 5 million.

This may seem a low probability but, looked at another way, it says that the bank would not lose more than USD 5 million in trading on more than $2^1/_2$ days in a year. This assumes that there are approximately 250 days a year when the markets are open for trading. In practice $2^1/_2$ days would be rounded up to three days as profit and loss is calculated daily. This result (2½ days) is an approximation and depends on a number of factors, such as the accuracy of the model. Notwithstanding these and other shortcomings, this calculation and the value it yields give very clear insight into measuring risk levels in different portfolios and in different banks. VaR thus represents a major step forward for both management and supervisors trying to understand the risks a bank was running in its trading businesses.

A bank with a higher VaR is running a higher level of risk. For instance, if Bank A has a VaR of USD 10 million at the 99% confidence level while Bank B has a VaR of USD 5 million at the same confidence level, then Bank A is running twice the risk of Bank B, as measured by VaR. Inevitably the use of VaR led the senior management of banks to ask a further question: "So how bad could the bank's losses be in those $2^1/_2$ days?"

The response to this question depends on the risk the bank is taking, and is answered by calculation of economic capital.

4.2.2 Economic Capital Methodology

The answer is not simple because it depends on two complicating factors. First, the losses are typically unexpected and unlikely, and the more unlikely the event, the less data there are to support any analysis. Second, a combination of poor data and a need to predict very infrequent events requires more complex statistical modeling techniques, which are inherently prone to errors and simplifications.

VaR gives no indication of the actual losses that will occur beyond the specified confidence level (in this example, 99%) on a daily basis. Bank A is running twice the VaR, and hence the risk, of Bank B. However, it does not automatically follow that Bank A will lose twice as much as Bank B when losses exceed the 99% confidence level. Bank A's losses may be less, the same, or more than twice those of Bank B, because the losses beyond the 99% confidence level could differ significantly for each bank, and may not be known prior to the estimation of risk or economic capital.

It will also be evident that for many banks it is important that the answer to the "extent of losses" question should cover all the risks the bank is running, including credit, operational, and other risks, not just those risks that stem from its trading portfolio. For many commercial banks this also means measuring potential losses from corporate and/or retail loans, as these credit risks are often the largest source of potential loss. In addition, it means considering other risks such as those being run through their operations areas, i.e., operational risk.

The most sophisticated banks have developed models that measure the potential extreme and unexpected losses in scenarios that involve losses from a combination of their market risk (including that held in the banking book—see Chapter 1), credit risk, operational risk, and other risks.

These models then estimate the capital necessary for the bank to survive worst-case losses from a combination of these risk areas.

4.2.3 Problems with Measuring Economic Capital

The diagram in Figure 4.1 is commonly used to highlight a number of the issues in understanding economic capital models.

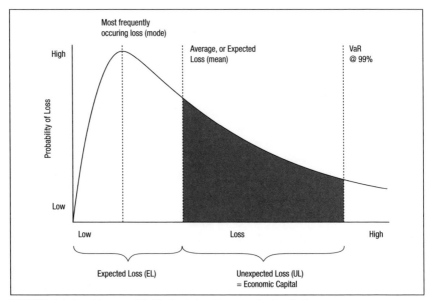

FIGURE 4.1: Problems with Underlying Economic Capital

The diagram above illustrates several important points:

- It represents (an assumed) statistical distribution of the potential losses a bank might sustain over a future time period, for example one year.
- It is skewed: the range of possible losses (not the cumulative amount) above the average (mean) is much greater than those below the average.
- The loss that is most likely to occur (the mode) is below the average (mean) loss.
- The Economic Capital is equal to VaR less the cumulative value of Expected Losses.

Important conclusions can be drawn from the diagram. These are:

- In most years the bank would look more profitable than it will be on average as its most likely loss (mode) is below the level of the average (mean).
- When loss levels are high they are really high, i.e., bad years don't come along very often but when they do, beware!

- A sufficiently well-capitalized bank (i.e., capitalized to survive bad years) will look over-capitalized most of the time, in the sense that most of its capital will appear to have been unused.

The explanation for the above conclusions is relatively simple to understand, in that:

- Losses for most commercial banks are dominated by credit losses and occur in large amounts only when the whole economy goes into recession, and the bank suffers losses in its corporate and retail lending books at the same time. (Few banks have broad geographical diversification of their business across many economies.)
- Many commercial banks have high concentrations of risk, both for geographical as well as historical reasons. A bank could have strong relationships in a certain part of the country or with a particular industry. For example, many banks with origins as mortgage lenders are very reliant on the economic prospects of the housing market.

It is the insight these models give to portfolio concentration risks that is of particular interest to supervisors. In fact, many supervisors have expressed concern that Basel II-based credit grading models do not provide adequate information in the area of concentration risk management.

4.2.4 Model Problems: Data

The data available to populate and therefore measure such distributions of losses are difficult to assemble. There are a number of reasons for this. Chief among them is that they require the bringing together of significantly different measures of risk.

Losses from trading can be easily updated on a daily basis and there are thousands of transactions per day, of which a significant number are likely to produce losses. As a result, a year of daily data will provide a good history from which a VaR model for market risk is derived.

In contrast, the transactions on which credit losses are based are undertaken much less often than trading transactions. They also last much longer, which means losses are less frequently observed. For these reasons, credit losses are usually assessed using annual loss data. Note that if historical data were used the model would require 100 years of back data to establish the loss at 99%, so other techniques have to be used.

It is difficult to populate operational risks models with data especially because some operational risks are difficult to quantify in financial loss terms. In practice the capital requirements are usually assessed over an annual period, in the same way as they are for credit risk. However, as with credit risk the difficulty of assembling sufficient historical data means that other statistical measurement techniques are commonly used.

4.2.5 Adding Up Economic Capital

The different categories of risk under Basel II (market, credit, and operational risk) all share a common development. For each category of risk, a computation similar to the one shown in Figure 4.1 is performed. In each case, the measure of capital is the difference between a measure of the maximum likely loss and the expected loss. While the maximum likely loss is called "VaR" for market risk and "Unexpected Loss" for credit risk, the result is the same.

As the capital is diversified across market, credit, and operational risk, bankers may ask why the aggregate capital is computed as the sum of the three capital measures, instead of a sum adjusted for a diversification benefit. In theory, the risk of the sum should be less than the sum of the risks.

In practice, it would be very difficult for banks to estimate the correlations between the risk categories and any resulting diversification benefit. Regulators would not be able to assert a standard because the correlations would be different for banks with different activity levels. For example, the correlation between market capital and credit capital would be different for a bank that focuses on trading and for one that focuses on lending.

Therefore, practitioners use the most conservative assumption possible: they assume that all risks are perfectly correlated, and simply add the risk measures.

4.2.6 Supervisory Acceptance of Economic Capital Models

Supervisors following the principles of the Basel II Accord are tasked with an oversight responsibility of the various internal capital adequacy models estimating the economic capital of banks. In this capacity, supervisors need to ensure that the models comply with regulatory pronouncements, and address several concerns. These concerns stretch from data issues, such as the quality, relevance, and adequacy of data available in the models and the input into these models, to the relative newness of such models that make verification difficult. Additionally, there may be concerns related to timing differences. Operational risks and operational risk capital are often assessed on an annual basis as are credit risks and credit risk capital. But market risks are assessed on a more frequent basis and can focus on such short time periods as one day, one week, or 10 trading days. It is not only adding up the risks and the required risk capital across different time frequencies that causes problems; the potential correlation across these risks are difficult to quantify and are generally poorly understood.

The timing and measuring of differences leads to final complexity that regulators and banks have been trying to resolve. The various models ultimately support decisions on retaining capital. The methods of measuring very unlikely and infrequently occurring loss events can be difficult to understand. For example, how would a bank react if the likelihood of a certain level of extreme loss has risen from 0.05% (5 in 10,000 or 1 in 2,000) to 0.1% (1 in 1,000)? Differently put, how would the capital requirements change if the likelihood of a loss event increases from once every 8 years to once every 4 years? Should the bank raise more capital or ignore it?

A number of sophisticated banks do use economic capital models to support decisions regarding the level and structure of capital they believe they should hold. They are also used for pricing transactions against the likely level of loss the bank could sustain over time. Additionally, such models give valuable insight into a bank's portfolio concentration risk. Some major banks even publish the results from their economic capital models in their annual accounts, attesting to their importance in helping management make decisions relating to capital and risk.

Given the widespread use of such models, supervisors cannot ignore them. Under Pillar 2 of the Basel II Accord, banks using such models are expected to share and discuss their results with supervisors. There are also requirements for sophisticated banks to develop methodologies to look at capital in relation to their own risk estimates. Such methodologies may and often do involve the development and use of economic capital models.

4.3 Components of Regulatory Capital

While the provisions of the Basel Accords are voluntary, nearly every major jurisdiction has embraced them, though jurisdictions have been free to choose certain parameters, such as the timing of the adoption of the capital rules. For students unfamiliar with Basel I and Basel II, a review of the Foundations of Financial Risk (FFR) material is recommended.

This section covers the details about what is considered capital for the purposes of regulatory calculations.

4.3.1 Bank Capital

In the FRR, eligible capital was defined as shareholders' equity and bank-issued bonds that are structured so that they qualify as "debt capital." Debt capital can best be defined as capital that will be repaid—if the bank goes into liquidation—after depositors and other debt holders of the bank have been repaid, but before equity capital holders. For this reason it is known as subordinated debt. (It is "subordinated" to the claims of the bank's depositors and other lenders to the bank.) Equity capital constitutes fully paid ordinary shares/common stock and non-cumulative perpetual preferred shares/stock. (The terms "stocks" and "shares" are, for the purposes of this chapter, interchangeable. Hereafter only shares will be used in the text.)

The capital of a bank, subject to Basel standards, can be described as having two major tiers: Tier 1 and Tier 2, plus one additional tier which has a very restricted use, Tier 3 (Tier 3 was introduced in Basel II and phased out under Basel III). A bank's capital structure becomes more complicated when considering how capital is created and the variety of debt and equity instruments that capital markets can originate.

4.3.2 Tier 1 Capital

The Basel Committee considers that the key element of capital on which supervisors should place the most emphasis is equity capital. Added to this is profits that have been accrued to reserves. Together these two elements constitute core capital.

To this core capital a bank can add what is often called "innovative" Tier 1 capital to create its total Tier 1 capital. Innovative Tier 1 structures are capital market instruments which, in terms of repayment, are ranked between shareholders' equity and debt, and which have features of both. As these innovative capital products are subordinated to debt issued by the bank, they are typically structured as preferred stock. Supervisors place strict rules on the features of such market instruments and the extent to which they can be issued.

Tier 1 capital also includes certain disclosed reserves. Disclosed reserves are typically those reserves that are created using the bank's after-tax income.

4.3.3 Tier 2 Capital

Tier 2 capital comprises debt capital that is subordinated (to the interests of depositors and other creditors) in the event of a bank going into liquidation, but is not subordinated to equity and innovative capital products that would count as Tier 1 capital. However, it excludes perpetual non-cumulative preference shares, which are typically used as one of the innovative capital products.

Because the liquidation of any company usually results in not all of its creditors being repaid from the liquidation of the company's assets, the ranking of creditors for repayment on default (i.e., who gets paid first, second, etc.) is very important. While debt capital holders will be paid prior to shareholders, they will only be paid after depositors and other creditors. Therefore the holders of debt capital will be the last creditors to be paid following a liquidation (prior to any distribution to Tier 1 capital instrument holders). Shareholders, as owners, are not creditors of the company they own. Any residual value in a liquidation—following payments to all creditors—is the property of equity investors.

Banks often classify the components of their Tier 2 capital into an upper and lower Tier 2 capital. Upper Tier 2 capital is distinguished from other subordinated debt issues that pay interest (and where failure to do so would be an event of default). Upper Tier 2 capital comprises:

- Preference shares (technically a form of debt) that confer on issuers the right to defer payment of a fixed dividend. Because the dividend is a fixed percentage of the debt, in most circumstances it is similar in nature to an interest payment.
- General provisions comprising provisions against loan losses which may reasonably be expected to happen (within the next year), but which cannot be related to a specific default. It should be noted that the inclusion of general provisions is subject to a limit of 1.25% of risk-weighted assets under the Standardized Approach to credit risk. If expected loss (EL) is greater than the total provisions then 50% of the difference is deducted from each of Tier 1 and Tier 2 capital. If EL is less than the provisions the difference is reflected in Tier 2 capital.
- Certain revaluation reserves, i.e., an increase in capital resulting from the revaluation of certain assets such as real estate also belong in this category of capital.

■ Certain hybrid debt capital instruments which are similar to equity and which must include the ability to support ongoing losses without triggering liquidation.

Lower Tier 2 capital includes subordinated debt issues that pay interest. It must have a maturity on initial issue of at least five years. Of the amount issued only:

■ 80% of outstanding debt can count as Tier 2 capital four years before repayment
■ 60% can count three years before repayment
■ 40% can count two years before repayment
■ 20% can count one year before repayment

4.3.4 Tier 3 Capital

Tier 3 capital was a form of Basel II debt capital that could only be used to support market risk in the trading book of the bank. It comprised subordinated debt that was issued initially for a minimum of two years. In addition, debt repayments on Tier 3 debt capital had to be suspended if the bank's capital fell below its individual capital ratio as set by its national supervisor.

This capital tier was introduced with Basel II in 2004 and withdrawn with Basel III in 2010.

4.3.5 Options on Capital Instruments

There are also restrictions on the attachment of options to all debt capital instruments used for capital purposes. If the purchaser has an option to demand repayment before the debt's scheduled repayment date (a put option), the option date will count as the repayment date for capital purposes. If the issuer has the right to repay before the scheduled repayment date (a call option), it will be ignored for capital purposes, unless the issuer is due to pay a higher rate of interest as compensation to the holder for not having exercised the option (known as a step-up clause).

4.3.6 Deductions from Capital

When calculating regulatory capital following the rules laid down in the Basel II framework, deductions are typically made for goodwill, investments made in subsidiaries, and the bank's equity holdings of other banks. Each of these topics is explored in sequence.

Goodwill deduction
Goodwill can often be seen as a capital item in company balance sheets. It arises as a result of the purchase of a business for more than the value of the capital of the acquired company as it is valued in that company's balance sheet. The excess payment to the shareholders of the acquired company becomes goodwill in the new consolidated balance sheet of the acquiring and acquired companies.

Under both Basel I and II, Tier 1 capital is subjected to a number of adjustments. One important adjustment is the deduction of any goodwill item in the balance sheet. The balance sheet of the new (acquired plus acquiring) bank will, depending on the size of the goodwill payment made to the acquired bank's shareholders, have less Tier 1 capital than that which the banks independently had before the acquisition. Because the purpose of acquisition is often to grow the business the reduced Tier 1 capital may well lead to the need to issue new shares.

Investments in subsidiaries
Investments in subsidiaries engaged in banking and similar activities, where the subsidiary is not consolidated into the regulated banking group's balance sheet, will result in a deduction from capital of the book value of the equity investment.

Holding of shares in another bank
In a number of countries it is common for a bank to have its capital reduced by the value of the shares it holds in other banks. This is subject to the discretion of the local supervisor.

4.3.7 Ratios Between Tiers of Capital

In the Basel II Accord, the Basel Committee set out rules for the ratios that banks should maintain between different classes of equity. The primary restriction is that Tier 2 capital cannot exceed 50% of a bank's total regulatory capital. Furthermore, innovative instruments in Tier 1 are limited to a maximum of 15% of Tier 1 capital after deductions are made, and the lower Tier 2 capital, typically consisting of subordinated debt issues, may only equal up to 50% of total capital. Additionally local supervisors often impose a wider range of additional ratio requirements between different tiers and sub-tiers of capital.

4.3.8 Basel III Capital Rules

The Basel III proposal in 2010 included not only a redefinition of several key capital components compared to Basel II, but also introduced several additional measures of capital. Coming shortly after the global financial crisis of 2007-2009, Basel III comprised tough new capital requirements.

No more Tier 3
When Basel II was introduced in 2004 it was thought that banks would be interested in separating their trading activities and capitalizing them separately. This never truly occurred, perhaps because of a limitation whereby Tier 3 capital could not exceed 250% of the portion of Tier 1 capital reserved for market risk: a bank with capital of 100 (in USD), using 95 for credit risk and 5 for market risk, would be allowed an additional 12.5 units of Tier 3 capital. This capital could be provided through subordinated debt of a bank, with an original maturity of at least two years and subject to a lock-in that would prohibit interest and principal payments, even at maturity, if the bank was below its regulatory minimum capital level. Consequently, the investor appetite for Tier 3 bonds was not enthusiastic.

This rather complicated affair was removed from Basel III, as the quality of this type of capital was not considered sufficiently high.

Core Tier 1 (Going Concern)
In addition to the previous overall capital adequacy ratio, Basel III introduced a renewed emphasis on Tier 1 capital, now referred to as Core Tier 1 and Additional Tier 1 ratios. Tier 1 was previously defined as "at least" half the overall capital requirement, or 4%. The new minimum percentage for Core Tier 1 is 4.5%, and was due to take effect by January 1, 2015. Core Tier 1 consists of paid-up common stock in the bank, share premium, retained earnings, and disclosed reserves.

Additional Tier 1
This is an add-on layer to Core Tier 1 and takes total Tier 1 capital up to a new 6% requirement.

Additional Tier 1 consists of instruments issued by the bank which are subordinated to everything except common stock. Characteristics of such instruments are: they are not secured or guaranteed; they are perpetual with no incentives to redeem; if they are callable, they may be called only after at least five years; their repayment or redemption may be made only with supervisory approval; the bank retains discretion to distribute coupons/ dividends; they are convertible bonds with put features in favor of the bank; they comprise conditional convertible bonds (CoCo's).

Tier 1 Capital
This is the sum of Core Tier 1 and Additional Tier 1 capital and must be at least 6% at all times.

Tier 2 (Gone Concern)
Consists of instruments issued by the bank which are subordinated to everything except Tier 1 capital. It may have similar characteristics to Additional Tier 1 capital plus dated subordinated debt.

Total Capital
This is the sum of Tier 1 and Tier 2 capital and is 8%, as before, although, given the capital buffers described below, this number is more for historical reference than a reflection of new capital requirements.

Capital Buffers
Several new capital buffers were introduced by Basel III: Capital Conservation Buffer, Countercyclical Buffer, and a special SIFI Buffer.

The Capital Conservation Buffer will be 2.5% when applied 100% in 2019.

The Countercyclical Buffer may range from 0% to 2.5% at the discretion of national supervisors.

The special SIFI Buffer comes in five buckets from 1% to 3.5% and SIFI banks are allocated to one corresponding to the required level of additional loss absorbency. Initially, there are no SIFI's in the 3.5% Bucket 5.

See also Basel III: A global regulatory framework (June 2011), http://www.bis.org/publ/bcbs189.pdf

4.3.9 Basel III Leverage Rules

Prior to Basel III, there were no explicit leverage rules applicable to banks. Implicitly, it was assumed that the 8% Capital Adequacy Ratio would put an automatic damper on leverage of 12.5 times equity. This turned out to be very far from reality. For example, in 2008, Lehman Brothers had a leverage ratio of around 30 times equity at its default. Many other banks had similar leverage ratios at that time.

In response to the recriminations that followed, the Basel Committee introduced a measure for non-risk-weighted leverage to be applied by banks under Basel III. The formula for the Leverage Ratio within Basel III is:

$$\text{Leverage Ratio} = \frac{\text{Tier 1 Capital}}{\text{Total Expenditure}} \geq 3\%$$

The exposure measure in the formula follows the accounting measure and there are therefore no adjustments for risk weights, as there are for capital adequacy calculations. This is, in fact, the whole purpose of the Leverage Ratio: to avoid the masking of the true ratio via the risk weights. The result, however, reveals a startling fact: by inverting the 3% into a real ratio, i.e., 100/3, we find that the Basel Committee condones a leverage ratio of 33 times equity. This is roughly the same number banks had at the beginning of the global credit crisis of 2007-2009, and, for many, that meant they had to be bailed out by governments.

With the renewed Basel III focus on Tier I capital, which must now be 6%, up from 4% under Basel II, it could be argued that 17 times (100/6) leverage should be the maximum acceptable at banks. However, by using 3%, essentially half the Tier 1 minimum capital allowed, the Basel Committee is signalling that they believe risk weightings in bank's asset portfolios are, on average, 50%.

The Leverage Ratio will not be in full force until January 1, 2018.

4.3.10 The Capital Creation Process

Banks raise new equity capital for a variety of reasons and in a number of ways. The main reasons for raising a large amount of new capital are as a result of:

■ The write-off of loans destroying existing capital and thus requiring new capital to support the bank's remaining business, or
■ Senior management asking existing and potential shareholders to support a strategy of rapid growth in the balance sheet through either new business generation or a proposed acquisition.

4.3.11 Acquisitions and Capital

The reason banks often need to issue capital after making an acquisition is that the acquiring bank usually needs to pay a premium to the acquired bank.

It should be noted that when the acquisition is being made the shareholders and markets will be more concerned with the premium to the current share price of the target bank. This premium should not be confused with the book value of the shareholders' equity which is relevant to bank capital for regulatory purposes.

4.3.12 Capital and Profits

Banks that are profitable create a flow of new capital on a continuing basis, as profits after bad debt and other provisions are available to be added to its Tier 1 capital base. (Alternatively, such profits can be distributed to shareholders, but in that case they do not result in any increase in the bank's capital.) These retained profits are called "retentions." Retentions allow the bank to support new business without needing to ask shareholders for new capital. Raising capital through the shareholders is a process that, if carried out on a regular basis, is time consuming and expensive.

The process of adding to a bank's Tier 1 capital through retentions is carried out on an annual basis when its shareholders approve the bank's audited report and accounts, as recommended by the bank's senior management. In practice one of the most important approvals that shareholders give relates to the distribution of profits. The distribution can be divided between profits to be retained as new capital, and those returned to shareholders in the form of dividends.

While the reporting process is, by law, usually done on an annual or semiannual basis (although quarterly reporting is the accepted practice in the US and is used by some companies in certain other jurisdictions) the process of profit creation is continuous. The Basel Committee recognizes this by allowing audited interim profits, net of any anticipated tax and dividends, to be included in Tier 1 capital subject to approval by the bank's auditors. This is particularly useful for banks with rapidly growing businesses and, consequently, a rapidly growing balance sheet. If they were forced to wait for a full year before retained profits became available as capital, banks might need to raise interim injections of capital from shareholders to maintain their business growth.

4.3.13 JPMorgan Chase's Regulatory Capital

Risk-based capital ratios December 31	2013	2012
Capital ratios		
Tier 1 capital	11.9%	12.6%
Total capital	14.4%	15.3%
Tier 1 leverage	7.1%	7.1%
Tier 1 common[a]	10.7%	11.0%
(a) The Tier 1 common ratio is Tier 1 common capital divided by RWA.		
December 31, 2013 (in millions, except ratios)		
Tier 1 common under Basel I rules	$ 148,887	
Adjustments related to AOCI for AFS securities and defined benefit pension and OPEB plans	1,474	
Addback of Basel I deductions[a]	1,780	
Deduction for deferred tax asset related to net operating loss and foreign tax credit carryforwards	(741)	
All other adjustments	(198)	
Estimated Tier 1 common under Basel III rules	$ 151,202	
Estimated risk-weighted assets under Basel III Advanced Approach[b]	$ 1,590,873	
Estimated Tier 1 common ratio under Basel III Advanced Approach[c]		9.5%
(a) Certain exposures, deducted from capital under Basel I, are risk-weighted under Basel III.		
(b) RWA under Basel III Advanced Approach is on a fully phased-in basis. Effective January 1, 2013, market risk RWA requirements under Basel 2.5 became largely consistent across Basel I and Basel III.		
(c) The Tier 1 common ratio under Basel III rules is Tier 1 common divided by RWA under Basel III Advanced Approach.		

FIGURE 4.2 JPMorgan Chase's Regulatory Capital

The following chart presents the Basel III minimum risk-based capital ratios during the transitional periods and on a fully phased-in basis. The chart also includes management's target for the Firm's Tier 1 common ratio. It is the Firm's current expectation that its Basel III Tier 1 common ratio will exceed the regulatory minimums, both during the transition period and upon full implementation in 2019 and thereafter.

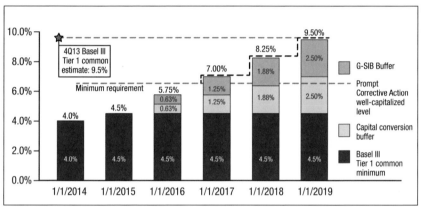

FIGURE 4.3 JPMorgan Chase Basel III Target Tier 1 Capital Ratio

The JPMorgan Chase report is particularly useful since it shows regulatory capital and compliance with all the relevant ratios discussed above.

4.4 Risk and Return for Financial Instruments

In classical finance theory, corporations were advised to undertake business activities as long as the expected return exceeded the minimum return required by well-diversified shareholders. A well-diversified shareholder has assets spread across a large group of different investments and would typically not suffer substantial losses if one or a few of the individual investments failed. If corporations followed this advice blindly, they might find themselves taking unduly high risks, a situation that would be remedied by recapitalizing the corporation to absorb the increased risk. Failing to recapitalize, the corporation would increase its risk of bankruptcy.

Banks cannot afford to follow the classical finance advice, since they are required by regulation to maintain risk levels within their current capitalization. They must have enough equity to sustain losses at conservatively estimated levels. Because of this, every risky transaction the bank enters uses up some of the bank's limited risk capacity. In order to ensure that the limited risk capacity is used wisely, banks put a cost on risk. Each transaction must earn not only the minimum return required by shareholders, but an additional return due to the expense of risk.

4.4.1 Risk-Adjusted Return on Capital (RAROC) of a Single Transaction

The most widely used measure of the cost of risk is RAROC, or the Risk-Adjusted Return on Capital, first developed by Bankers Trust in the late 1970s. On a forward-looking basis, RAROC is defined to be the following ratio:

$$\textit{Forward-looking RAROC} =$$
$$\textit{[Expected Profit Net of All Financing Costs] / Value-at-Risk}$$

At Bankers Trust in the 1990s, the VaR was computed at the 99% confidence level for one year, and a threshold RAROC of 25% was used. This implied that any deal done by the bank had to have an expected net profit that exceeded 25% of its VaR.

EXAMPLE

Bankers Trust has an opportunity to do a securitization deal for a credit card company, but has to retain a portion of the residual risk of the deal with an estimated VaR of USD 10 million. Its fees for the deal are USD 3 million, and the short-term financing costs are USD 600,000.

Profitability net of financing is USD 2.4 million, or 24% RAROC (while the risk charges are USD 2.5 million), but should have been at least 25%, or profits net of financing of at least USD 2.5 million. The deal will have to be restructured in order to increase profitability by at least 1% or to reduce the residual risk to at most USD 9.6 million. This could be accomplished by raising the fees, hedging the transaction or selling a portion of the residual risk to an outside buyer.

RAROC allows analysts to convert a measure of risk into a measure of cost and converts qualitative tradeoffs between return and risk into a quantitative tradeoff that can be rigorously enforced throughout a bank. By enforcing this discipline, the bank can ensure that each of its departments is considering the cost of risk in exactly the same way, and deciding how to structure and accept transactions within the same risk appetite guidelines.

Regulatory Capital Adjustment

Certain products might require a higher level of regulatory capital than expected relative to their risk. In these cases, projects must be subject to an incremental excess regulatory capital charge to ensure that projects do not foreclose other opportunities that use regulatory capital more efficiently. A surplus regulatory capital charge can be deducted from the numerator in the RAROC calculation.

VaR as a Measure of Capital

The RAROC equation in the last section may seem peculiar to analysts who would expect returns to be measured on the basis of cash investment. Indeed, the risks of many types of investments can be measured in this way. For example, an investor in a junk bond may expect to lose as much as his cash investment in the bond, but not more. However, bank transactions can be extremely complex, and require little to no cash. Despite requiring no cash, they have the potential to require additional cash in the future, unlike a junk bond investment. For this reason, it is more relevant to a bank to consider the range of possible future cash outlays associated with an investment rather than merely its initial cash outlay.

EXAMPLE

The bank takes a long position in the oil futures market that requires a 2% margin, i.e., the bank has to deposit 2% of the value of the contract with the broker. The futures contracts were priced at USD 60 per barrel (bbl) at inception, and rose by USD 3 to USD 63. The VaR on the position is estimated to be USD 10.

The return would seem to be 5%, or 3/60. However, the bank only paid 2% of USD 60 or USD 1.20 in margin per bbl. Alternatively, then, the return on investment is the return on the margin, which is 250%, or 3/1.20. This is also incorrect, since the bank could lose more than USD 1.20/bbl on the contract if the price declines.

The best answer is to determine the maximum likely future cash outlay, the reasonably expected loss on the position. This can be estimated by a VaR calculation. By linking VaR, the reasonably expected loss on the position, to the realized profit, the risk and the returns are captured. Thus, the risk-adjusted return, RAROC, is 30% = 3/10.

In summary, those who measure return on investment do so because cash is a scarce commodity and needs to be allocated wisely to those investments that provide the overall highest cash return. Those who measure return on risk (RAROC) do so because cash is relatively plentiful and risk is the scarce commodity. In many bank transactions, VaR is a better measure of capital than the initial cash outlay.

4.4.2 Combining Financial Instruments Into Portfolios

In the RAROC discussion above, we analyzed the case of a single bank transaction. In that example, the VaR of a stand-alone transaction was USD 10 million. However, since the bank runs a large portfolio with a large number of transactions, the actual risk to the bank of the transaction is less than USD 10 million. The reason for this is diversification. As a bank invests in transactions with different kinds of risks, it can expect to enjoy a diversification benefit from investing in new transactions. The lower the correlation, the greater the diversification benefit. If the correlation between a new transaction and the bank's portfolio is negative, the transaction is called a hedge of the bank's portfolio risks.

EXAMPLE

The bank's VaR is USD 100 million prior to the transaction mentioned above. If the new transaction correlates perfectly with the bank's current risks, there is no diversification benefit: the total VaR of the bank rises to USD 110 million. If the correlation of the new transaction with the bank portfolio is zero, the incremental risk is negligible, only USD 0.5 million. If the new transaction hedges the bank's current risk perfectly, at a correlation of −1, the bank risk, after the transaction, falls to USD 90 million.

The chart below shows how the diversification benefit depends on the correlation between the new transaction and the existing bank portfolio: diversification benefits increase the lower the correlation.

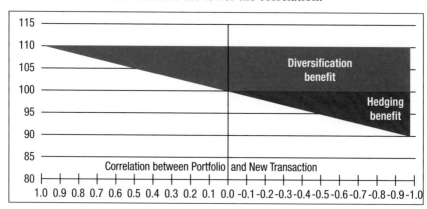

FIGURE 4.4 Portfolio VaR with New Transaction

The relationship is not exactly linear, though the graph may suggest that in this instance, as a straight line approximates the relationship. The exact formula is:

$$New\ Bank\ VaR =$$
$$\sqrt{[Bank\ VaR^2 + Transaction\ VaR^2}$$
$$+\ (2 \times correlation \times Bank\ VaR \times Transaction\ VaR)]$$

If the correlation between the new transaction and the existing bank portfolio is 0.25, the new bank VaR is $\sqrt{[100^2 + 10^2 + (2 \times 0.25 \times 100 \times 10)]}$ = USD 102.96 million.

In most banks, the diversification benefit is assumed to accrue to the bank, not to the transaction. One argument for this is that correlation is rarely certain, therefore the bank effectively assumes perfect correlation amongst its transactions in order to be conservative. In a crisis situation, such as the global credit crisis of 2007-9, this may not have been a bad assumption, as seemingly unrelated markets all moved dramatically at the same time. A second reason for this assumption is that the bank can pass on some of its expected diversification benefit by reducing the cost of risk to its business units. This would imply, for example, that the bank may require an overall RAROC of 35%, but charges its business lines 25% knowing that it will achieve some diversification benefit.

4.4.3 Portfolio Return and Risk

Suppose a bank department wishes to know how portfolios of transactions affect its overall risk level. If every transaction has a profitability of USD 1 million before risk charges, and a VaR of USD 10 million, it would appear that each transaction by itself would not satisfy the bank's RAROC criteria. However, the story changes if the transactions are not perfectly correlated. In this case, the risk increases as more transactions are completed, but the risk rises more slowly than the profitability. The graph below illustrates how transaction volume increases RAROC through diversification. All transactions are assumed to be identically structured, with identical correlations.

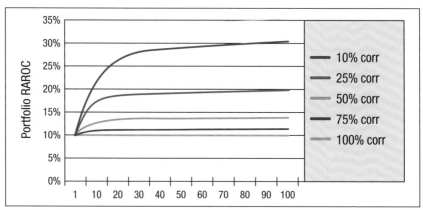

FIGURE 4.5 Transaction Volume Impact on RAROC

The maximum multiple of RAROC achievable is equal to the multiplicative inverse of the square root of the correlation. For example, if the transactions have a common correlation of 0.25, the maximum RAROC multiple is $1/\sqrt{0.25} = 2$. Raising the RAROC from 10% to 20% will still not meet the bank's criteria for profitability. In this case, with 25% correlation, each transaction must have an individual RAROC of 12.5% to meet a total department threshold of 25%, and the department must expect to do at least 100 transactions. Alternatively, the department would have to find other risk mitigating alternatives to make the department successful in RAROC terms.

In summary, portfolios of transactions will generally show a higher RAROC than the average of the transaction RAROCs. This is because even a small amount of diversification benefit allows the portfolio VaR to grow at a slower rate than portfolio profitability.

4.4.4 Estimates of JPMorgan Chases's RAROC

Given the development in the last two sections, it may seem reasonable to expand the RAROC framework to evaluate the performance of all the business units of a bank. We can see how this exact objective has been accomplished at JPMorgan Chase.

In its 2013 Annual Report, JPMorgan Chase states (p. 165):

"The Firm's framework for allocating capital to its business segments is based on the following objectives:

- *Integrate firmwide and line of business capital management activities*
- *Measure performance consistently across all lines of business*
- *Provide comparability with peer firms for each of the lines of business*

Equity for a line of business represents the amount the Firm believes the business would require if it were operating independently, considering capital levels for similarly rated peers, regulatory capital requirements (as estimated under Basel III), and economic risk measures. Capital is also allocated to each line of business for, among other things, goodwill and other intangibles associated with acquisitions effected by the line of business. ROE is measured and internal targets for expected returns are established as key measures of a business segment's performance."

Line of business equity	Yearly average		
Year ended December 31 (in billions)	**2013**	**2012**	**2011**
Consumer & Community banking	$ 46.0	$ 43.0	$ 41.0
Corporate & Investment Banking	56.5	47.5	47.0
Commercial Banking	13.5	9.5	8.0
Asset Management	9.0	7.0	6.5
Corporate/Private Equity	71.4	77.4	70.8
Total common stockholder's equity	**$ 196.4**	**$ 184.4**	**$ 173.3**

FIGURE 4.6 Line of Business Equity

It is these levels of economic capital that determine the performance of each business line. On page 85 of the 2013 Annual Report, JPMorgan Chase shows the returns by business line, which are simply computed as the ratio of net income to economic capital:

The following table summarizes the business segment results for the periods indicated.

Year ends December 31	Total net revenue (in millions)			Total noninterest expense (in millions)			Pre-provision profit/ (loss) (in millions)		
	2013	2012	2011	2013	2012	2011	2013	2012	2011
Consumer & Community Banking(a)	$ 46,026	$ 49,884	$ 45,619	$ 27,842	$ 28,827	$ 27,631	$ 18,164	$ 21,057	$ 17,982
Corporate& Investment Bank	34,225	34,326	33,984	21,744	21,850	21,979	12,481	12,476	12,005
Commercial Banking	6,973	6,825	6,418	2,610	2,389	2,278	4,363	4,436	4,140
Asset Management	11,320	9,946	9,543	8,016	7,104	7,002	3,304	2,842	2,541
Corporate/Private Equity(a)	1,254	(1,091)	4,203	10,255	4,559	4,015	(9,001)	(5,650)	188
Total	$ 99,198	$ 99,890	$ 99,767	$ 70,467	$ 64,729	$ 62,911	$ 29,331	$ 35,161	$ 36,856

Year ended December 31	Provision For credit losses (in millions, except ratios)			Net income/(loss) (in millions, except ratios)			Return on equity (in millions, except ratios)		
	2013	2012	2011	2013	2012	2011	2013	2012	2011
Consumer & Community Banking	$ 335	$ 3,774	$ 7,620	$ 10,749	$ 10,551	$ 6,105	23%	25%	15%
Corporate & Investment Bank	(232)	(479)	(285)	8,546	8,406	7,993	15%	18%	17%
Commercial Banking	85	41	208	2,575	2,646	2,367	19%	28%	30%
Asset Management	65	86	67	2,031	1,703	1,592	23%	24%	25%
Corporate/Private Equity	(28)	(37)	(36)	(5,978)	(2,022)	919	NM	NM	NM
Total	$ 225	$ 3,385	$ 7,574	$ 17,923	$ 21,284	$ 18,976	9%	11%	11%

(a) The 2012 and 2011 data for certain income statement line items (predominantly net interest income, compensation, and non-compensation expense) were revised to reflect the transfer of certain technology and operations, as well as real estate-related functions and staff, from Corporate/Private Equity to CCB effective January 1, 2013.

FIGURE 4.7   Segment Results — Managed Basis

4.5 Risk-based Performance Measurement

RAROC calculations are used for three purposes:

1. To report past performance
2. To provide benchmarks for current products, activities, and businesses
3. To guide the bank in the reallocation of its capital

The performance chart immediately suggests that given the aggregate RAROC of the JPMorgan Chase businesses of 13%, each business should be able to earn that minimum return on its economic capital. Furthermore, within a business, e.g., card services, at a 21% RAROC, new projects and products must return at least USD 0.21 per USD 1.00 in incremental economic capital created.

The RAROC numbers are used to allocate capital in the future—the 23% return in asset management looks much higher than the investment bank return of 15%. Should JPM put economic capital to work in asset management at the expense of the investment bank? Perhaps, but perhaps not. The asset management group might have had a particularly good year that is not expected to be repeated. The asset management business may not be able to be increased at the same level of return. Finally, the investment banking business probably adds a lot of strategic value for the JPM franchise that is not captured in the RAROC calculations.

4.6 Summary

This chapter has introduced a number of key concepts and issues involved in capital management and treasury risk.

Types of Capital
- Debt capital can best be described as capital that will be repaid, should the bank go into liquidation, after depositors and other debt holders of the bank have been repaid, but before equity capital holders.
- Equity capital constitutes fully paid ordinary shares/common stock and non-cumulative perpetual preferred shares/stock.
- The capital of a bank, subject to Basel standards, can be described as having two major tiers: Tier 1 and Tier 2. A third type of capital, Tier 3, was abolished under Basel III.

- The Basel Committee considers that the key element of capital on which supervisors should place most emphasis is equity capital, to which should be added the accrual of profits to reserves. Together these two elements constitute core capital.
- Tier 2 capital comprises debt capital that is subordinated (to the interests of depositors and other creditors) in the event of a bank going into liquidation.
- Upper Tier 2 capital is distinguished from other subordinated debt issues that pay interest because failure to pay interest on Upper Tier 2 capital is not an event of default.
- Lower Tier 2 capital comprises subordinated debt issues that pay interest. Such issues must also have a repayment date which must be at least five years in the future at the time of initial issue and of which only 80% of outstanding debt can count as Tier 2 capital four years before repayment, 60% three years before repayment, 40% two years before repayment, and 20% one year before repayment.
- Tier 3 capital is debt capital that can only be used to support market risk in the trading book of the bank.
- If the issuer has the right to repay before the scheduled repayment date, the option will be ignored for capital purposes, unless the issuer is due to pay a higher rate of interest as compensation to the holder for not having exercised the option.

Deductions from Capital

- Goodwill can often be seen as a capital item in company balance sheets and arises as a result of the purchase of a business for more than the value of the capital of the acquired company as it is valued in that company's balance sheet.
- The balance sheet of the new (acquired plus acquiring) bank will, depending on the size of the goodwill payment made to the acquired bank's shareholders, have less Tier 1 capital than that which the banks independently had before the acquisition.
- Investments in subsidiaries engaged in banking and similar activities, where the subsidiary is not consolidated into the regulated banking group's balance sheet, will result in a deduction from capital of the book value of the equity investment.
- In a number of countries it is common for a bank to have its capital reduced by the value of the shares it holds in other banks.

Ratios Between Tiers of Capital
- The Basel Committee sets out rules for the ratios that banks should maintain between different classes of equity.
- The primary restriction under Basel II is that Tier 2 capital cannot exceed 50% of a bank's total regulatory capital.

The Capital Creation Process
- The main reasons banks raise new equity capital through large share issues are as a result of:
  - The write-off of loans destroying existing capital
  - Senior management asking existing and potential shareholders to support a strategy of rapid growth in the balance sheet through either new business generation or a proposed acquisition.
- When an acquisition is being made the shareholders and markets will be more concerned with the premium to the current share price of the target bank.
- Banks that are profitable create a flow of new capital on a continuing basis, as profits after bad debt and other provisions can be retained as capital or distributed to shareholders.

Economic Capital
- Economic capital is a measure of a bank's capital requirement that relates directly to the aggregate risk the bank is running.
- Value-at-risk (VaR) models represented a major step forward for both management and supervisors trying to understand the risks a bank was running in its trading businesses. A bank with a higher Value-at-risk (VaR) is running a higher level of risk.
- Banks have developed models that measure the potential extreme losses in scenarios that involved losses from a combination of their risks.
- Many supervisors have expressed concern that Basel II-based credit grading models do not provide adequate information in the area of concentration risk management.
- The data available to populate and therefore measure risk distributions of losses is difficult to assemble.
- Supervisors are often wary of accepting economic capital models as a basis for estimating regulatory capital for a combination of reasons.
- A number of sophisticated banks, however, use economic capital models to support decisions regarding the level and structure of capital that they believe they should hold.

- Under Pillar 2 of Basel II, banks using such models are expected to share and discuss their results with supervisors.

RAROC (Risk Adjusted Return on Capital)
- RAROC is the return to an activity as measured by its risk rather than its cash requirements. It is well-suited for banks, where risk is more important than cash.
- RAROC is computed as the expected profit or loss of an activity net of financing costs, divided by the risk measure.
- In some cases, regulatory charges are added to the numerator of the RAROC calculation.
- In theory, RAROC should be measured on an incremental basis, but in practice, RAROC is measured for individual transactions, portfolios, or bank business units.
- RAROC acts as a hurdle rate for risk-taking activities. Only activities that have RAROCs exceeding a minimum threshold are accepted.

Glossary

Asset and Liability Management (ALM) The Asset and Liability Management function in a bank manages the risks arising from asset and liability mismatches as well as the liquidity risk and interest rate risk in the bank's banking book.

Asset Liability Committee (ALCO) Asset Liability Committee is typically a committee of senior managers and board members tasked with executing and overseeing the bank's ALM activities.

Bank A bank is a financial intermediary that takes deposits, makes loans, arranges payments, holds a banking license, and is subject to regulatory supervision by a banking regulator.

Banking book The banking book of a bank is the portfolio of assets, primarily loans, a bank expects to hold until maturity. The term typically refers to the loans the bank underwrites.

Basel Accords The Basel Accords (Basel I Accord, the Market Risk Amendment, the Basel II Accord, and the Basel III Accord) are the cornerstones of international risk-based banking regulation, the results of a collaborative attempt by banking regulators from major developed countries to create a globally valid and widely applicable framework for banks and bank risk management.

Basel Committee on Banking Supervision (BCBS) The Basel Committee on Banking Supervision is the source of the Basel Accords, and a forum for regulatory cooperation between its member countries on banking supervision-related matters. It was established by central bank governors, and consists of senior representatives of bank supervisory authorities and central banks from major economies.

Basis point A basis point is one-hundredth of one percent, or 0.0001, or 0.01%.

Bid-ask-spread The bid-ask spread is the difference between the buy price or rate (bid) and sell price or rate (ask) of a financial instrument.

Board of directors The board of directors has the ultimate responsibility for the management and performance of a company, is responsible for its governance, and is elected by the shareholders.

Bond   A bond is a legally binding contract through which the borrower (also referred to as the issuer of the bond) borrows the principal, an amount specified in the bond, from an investor and in exchange pays a specified amount of interest (also referred as the coupon payment), usually at regular intervals, and at maturity repays the principal.

Capital adequacy   Capital adequacy is achieved when a bank's capital ratio meets or exceeds the minimum capital ratio, which under the Basel Accords is 8% of risk weighted assets. It can be satisfied with Tier 1 and Tier 2 capital (and Tier 3 capital, under Basel II). Tier 1 capital has to account for at least 4% of risk-weighted assets; the remainder can be satisfied through Tier 2 and, in the case of market risk capital, Tier 3 capital. National banking regulators can deviate from these minimum capital adequacy ratios. Under Basel III the percentages have changed. Common Equity Tier 1 must be at least 4.5% of risk-weighted assets at all times. Tier 1 Capital must be at least 6.0% of risk-weighted assets at all times. Total Capital (Tier 1 Capital plus Tier 2 Capital) must be at least 8.0% of risk-weighted assets at all times.

Capital requirement   Capital requirement determines the minimum capital amount that regulators require each bank to hold against its risk levels.

Capital   Capital denotes financial assets or the financial value of assets, such as cash, or the long-term financial contribution of investors in a corporation.

Central bank   A central bank is the principal monetary authority of a country or a group of countries, and may also exercise regulatory and supervisory responsibilities over other banks, arrange payment between banks and, when needed, provide stability to the financial and banking system.

Clearinghouse   A clearinghouse guarantees the financial performance of a trade on an exchange by becoming the buyer to each seller and the seller to each buyer; and it provides clearing and settlement services for financial transactions.

Collateral   Collateral is an asset pledged by a borrower to secure a loan or other credit and is forfeited to the lender in the event of the borrower's default.

Commercial bank   A commercial bank offers a wide range of highly specialized loans to large businesses, acts as an intermediary in raising funds, and provides specialized financial services including payment, investment, and risk management services.

Corporate governance   Corporate governance is a set of relationships between the board of directors, shareholders, and other stakeholders of an organization. It outlines the relationship between these groups, sets rules how the organization should be managed, and sets its operational framework.

Cost of funds   The cost of funds is the interest rate, required return, or other compensation associated with securing and using capital.

Counterparty   A counterparty is a party to a contract who is contractually bound and is expected to perform—deliver securities, make payments, etc.—sometime in the future.

Counterparty credit risk   Counterparty credit risk is the risk that the other party to a contract or agreement will fail to perform under the terms of an agreement, and is particularly relevant for trading.

Credit risk   Credit risk is the risk of loss due to non-payment of a loan, bond, or other credit.

Default   Default is the failure to pay interest or principal according to contractual terms. It occurs when a debtor or a counterparty is unable to make a timely payment or delivery.

Default risk   Default risk is the potential loss due to default.

Deposit   A deposit is money entrusted to a bank for safekeeping in a bank account that allows the depositor to withdraw these funds and any interest paid by the bank on the deposit.

Derivative   A (financial) derivative does not have an intrinsic value of its own. Its value changes in response to changes in the value of a related underlying financial asset or commodity, and includes swaps, options, forwards, and futures.

Disclosure   Disclosure is the dissemination of information about the conditions of a business that allows for a proper and transparent evaluation of that business.

Dividend   A dividend is the part of the earnings of a corporation that are paid out to its owners typically through the payment of cash or the issuance of additional shares.

Duration   Duration is a measure of price sensitivity for a fixed income instrument and quantifies the sensitivity of the price of a fixed-income investment to a small incremental change in interest rates.

Economic capital   Economic capital is the amount of capital a bank needs in the case of loss events. It covers all risks across a bank, and is essential for the bank to survive in the long term. It can be defined as VaR minus expected losses.

Endogenous Liquidity   Endogenous liquidity is the liquidity inherent in the banks' assets themselves.

Equity   Equity is the capital raised from shareholders and from retained earnings, and reflects the ownership interest in a corporation.

Equity capital   Equity capital is capital the bank has raised from shareholders and from its earnings.

Equity risk   Equity risk is the potential loss due to an adverse change in the price of stock.

Exchange   A (financial) exchange is a formal, organized physical or electronic marketplace where trades between investors follow standardized procedures.

Exogenous liquidity   Exogenous liquidity (often called funding liquidity) is the liquidity provided to a bank by its liability structure, including its ability to borrow and obtain contingent lines.

Exposure at Default (EAD)   Exposure at Default is the maximum loss a lender or counterparty may suffer in case of a default.

External liquidity   External liquidity is the noncontractual contingent capital supplied by investors and other institutions to support a bank during times of liquidity stress.

Fair market price   Fair market price is the price the asset would fetch if sold on the market immediately to a willing buyer.

Financial asset   A financial asset derives its value from a specific contractual claim and typically includes bonds, loans, stocks, money, currency, derivatives, certain commodities, and other assets of value.

Financial instrument   A financial instrument is a representation of an ownership interest claim or the contractual or contingent claim to receive or deliver cash, another financial instrument, or asset, and can either be a cash instrument (e.g., cash, securities, loans, bonds, notes, equity) or a derivative instrument (e.g., forward, future, option, and swap).

Fractional reserve banking   Fractional reserve banking is a banking system where only a small fraction of the total deposits must be held in reserve with the balance available to be invested in loans and other securities.

Funding liquidity risk   Funding liquidity risk refers to a bank's potential inability to have funds available to repay depositors on demand and to fund loans when needed.

Funds Transfer Pricing (FTP)   Funds Transfer Pricing. A method to separate the components of Net Interest Margin (NIM) into its constituent parts: Asset spread, Funding spread, and Liability spread.

Futures contract   A futures (contract), a derivative, is a standardized and transferable contract traded on an exchange that defines the delivery of a specified asset (e.g., commodities, currencies, bonds, or stocks) for a specified quantity, at a specified price, and on a specified future date.

General or systematic market risk   General, or systematic, market risk is the risk of an adverse movement in the market prices that are applied across a range of financial assets, including fixed income, loans, equity, and commodities.

Goodwill   Goodwill arises as a result of the purchase of a business for more than the value of the capital of the acquired company as it is valued in that company's balance sheet. The excess payment to the shareholders of the acquired company becomes goodwill in the new consolidated balance sheet of the acquiring and acquired companies.

Governance   Governance relates to the rules, processes, policies, and regulations outlining and defining the capacity, operational management, and administration of an organization, business, or other entity.

Hedging   Hedging reduces risk by matching a position as closely as possible with an opposite and offsetting position in a financial instrument that tracks or mirrors the value changes in the position.

HQLA   High Quality Liquid Assets is a term used as part of the BCBS Liquidity Coverage Ratio. They comprise Level 1, Level 2A, and Level 2B assets.

Hybrid security   A hybrid security is a financial instrument that has both equity and debt features.

Innovative capital   Innovative capital includes complex financial instruments that have both equity and debt features.

Insolvency   Insolvency occurs when liabilities exceed assets. While not synonymous with bankruptcy or illiquidity, it typically leads to either or both.

Interbank loan   An interbank loan is a loan between banks.

Interest rate   Interest rate, the price of credit, is the rate charged for accessing and using borrowed funds.

Interest rate risk   Interest rate risk is the potential loss of value due to the variability of interest rates.

Interest rate swap   An interest rate swap is a contractual agreement under which two parties exchange different types of interest payments on a predetermined amount for a known period of time with known frequency.

Interest-rate risk in the banking book   The interest rate risk in the banking book is caused by maturity differences between bank assets and liabilities, by differing interest rates used for pricing, and differing repricing points.

Internal Ratings Based (IRB) Approach The Internal Ratings Based approach to determine the regulatory minimum capital requirement for credit risk uses the bank's own information, and includes two different procedures that have methodological differences to forecast the different risk factors.

Junior debt Junior debt is subordinated to more senior debt in case of bankruptcy, default, or similar event, but has priority before equity.

Level 1 asset A type of HQLA that includes cash, central bank reserves, marketable securities issued by sovereigns, central banks, Public Sector Entities, the BIS itself, the IMF, the ECB, the European Community, and multilateral development banks. Such instruments must be assigned a 0% RWA weighting under Basel II Standardized Approach, meaning AAA to AA- rated. No haircuts are applied to Level 1 assets.

Level 2A asset A type of HQLA that includes marketable securities issued by sovereigns, central banks, PSEs, or multilateral development banks assigned a 20% RWA weighting under Basel II Standardized Approach, meaning A+ to A- rated. Also includes corporate debt, commercial paper, and covered bonds, as long as not issued by a financial institution and rated from AAA to AA-.

Level 2B assets A type of HQLA that includes residential Mortgage Backed Securities (75% haircut), with a maximum Loan-To-Value ratio of 80% and rated from AAA to AA. Also includes corporate bonds rated between A- and BBB- and exchange traded stocks in non-financial issues that are also constituents in a major domestic equity index (50% haircut). Level 2B assets may not account for more than 15% of the total stock of HQLAs, while Level 2A and 2B assets combined may not account for more than 40% of the total stock of HQLAs.

Leverage Leverage reflects the amount or proportion of debt used in the financing structure of an organization. The higher the leverage the more debt the company uses.

Leverage Ratio A BCBS standard that the ratio of Tier 1 capital to all assets (accounting based) must be more than 3%. This implies a 33.3 times leverage multiple (100/3).

LIBOR (London InterBank Offered Rate) LIBOR is a daily reference rate based on the average interest rate banks in London charge other banks, on the offer side of the transaction, when borrowing and lending.

Liquidity Liquidity refers to either market (transactional) or funding (payment) liquidity.

Liquidity Coverage Ratio (LCR) The Liquidity Coverage Ratio is a short-term measure of liquidity resilience introduced by the BCBS. The standard came into effect on January 1, 2015, although only with 60% effect. Full effect of 100% will be attained by 2019.

Liquidity risk Liquidity risk can be market (transactional) liquidity risk and funding (payment) liquidity risk.

Long position A long position, the opposite of short position, represents the ownership position of an asset. When the asset's value increases, the position's value increases and when the asset's value decreases, the position's value decreases.

Market liquidity risk Market liquidity risk refers to conditions when trading—buying and selling—assets significantly affects their transaction price or can only be executed at significant price concessions. Also called asset liquidity risk.

Market risk Market risk is defined as the risk of losses in on- and off-balance-sheet positions arising from movements in market prices, and typically encompasses the risks pertaining to interest rate related instruments and equities in the trading book, and foreign exchange risk and commodities risk throughout the bank.

Mark-to-market Marked-to-market (accounting) assigns a value to an asset that reflects the value it would fetch on the market.

Maturity Maturity is the time period until a loan, bond, or other credit is repaid fully.

Net interest income Net interest income is the difference between interest income and interest expense.

NSFR The Net Stable Funding Ratio is a medium-term (though supposedly long-term) measure of liquidity resilience introduced by the BCBS. The full measure will apply from 2019.

Operational risk Operational risk is the risk of loss resulting from inadequate or failed internal processes, people, and systems, or from external events. This definition includes legal risk, but excludes strategic and reputational risk.

Paid-in-capital Paid-in-capital is the (equity) capital that the owners have invested in a corporation.

Portfolio A portfolio is a collection of investments, such as stocks, bonds, and cash equivalents, held by an institution or a private individual.

Preferred share A preferred share has properties of both equity and debt. It is senior to common stock, but is subordinated to bonds. Usually it does not carry any voting rights.

Probabilistic model A probabilistic model incorporates the complex and interdependent behavior of complex assets and liabilities, and incorporates statistical and quantitative modeling.

PV01 The present value of a basis point, and, more specifically, the present value of 1 bp change in yield of an interest-bearing instrument. Also referred to as PVBP, DV01, or duration.

Rate Sensitive Assets (RSA) Rate sensitive assets are bank assets, mainly bonds, loans, and leases. The value of these assets is sensitive to changes in interest rates. They are either repriced or revalued as interest rates change.

Rate Sensitive Liabilities (RSL) Rate sensitive liabilities are bank liabilities, mainly interest-bearing deposits and other liabilities. The value of these liabilities is sensitive to changes in interest rates. They are either repriced or revalued as interest rates change.

Regulatory capital requirement Regulatory capital requirement specifies how much capital a bank must hold to guard against the various risks it takes, such as market risk, credit risk, and operational risk.

Repurchase agreement or repo A repurchase agreement, "repo," is a contract between two parties in which one party sells to the other a security at a specified price with the obligation to buy the security back at a later date for another specified price. They are widely used by central banks to provide support to meet banks' short-term liquidity needs.

Risk appetite Risk appetite is the level of risk exposure an investor is willing to assume in exchange for the potential for a profit.

Risk management Risk management is a structured approach to monitoring, measuring, and managing exposures to reduce the potential impact of an uncertain event happening.

Risk policy A risk policy outlines the risk management framework of an organization in relation to its objectives. It varies across and within industries and firms based on their ability to absorb losses and the rate of return they seek from operations.

Risk transfer Risk transfer is the assumption of specific risk for a fee, or premium.

Risk-Adjusted Return on Capital (RAROC) Risk-Adjusted Return on Capital adjusts the return generated by an asset for the inherent risk assumed by the project, so making it easier to compare and contrast projects with different risk profiles.

Risk-weighted assets (RWA) Risk-weighted assets equal the sum of various financial assets multiplied by their respective risk-weights as well as off-balance sheet items weighted for their credit risk according to the regulatory requirements outlined by banking regulators and supervisors.

Scenario analysis　Scenario analysis, or "what-if?" analysis, assesses the potential outcome of various scenarios by setting up several possible situations and analyzing the potential outcomes of each situation.

Securitization　Securitization is a process whereby illiquid cash flow producing assets (such as mortgages, credit cards, and loans, etc.) are pooled into a portfolio. The purchase of the assets in the portfolio is financed by securities issued to investors, who then share the cash flows generated by the portfolio.

Security　A (financial) security is a fungible financial instrument.

Senior bond　A Senior bond has priority over all other more junior and subordinated bonds in case of bankruptcy, default or similar event.

Shareholder　A shareholder, stockholder, or equity holder, is one of the owners of a corporation, and has the right to elect the board of directors, may decide in corporate matters, and may receive dividends.

Shareholder's equity　Shareholders' equity, the difference between assets and liabilities, is the shareholders' investment in the company, which typically equals the amount the shareholders have invested in the company and retained earnings.

Short position　A short position, the opposite of long position, represents either the selling of a borrowed asset, the writing of an option, or the selling of a futures position. When the asset's value increases, the position's value decreases and when the asset's value decreases, the position's value increases.

Solvency　Solvency denotes the financial condition of a firm when assets exceed liabilities.

Specific, non-systematic, firm-specific, unique risk　Specific, non-systematic, firm-specific, unique risk is the risk of an adverse movement in the price of one individual security or financial asset due to factors specific to that particular security or issuer.

Speculation　Speculation involves the buying (long position), holding, selling, and short-selling (short position) of financial assets, commodities, foreign exchange, or derivatives, in the expectation that price fluctuations will generate a profit. Speculation also refers to the holding of a position that is not hedged or when simply buying or selling an asset with the hope of earning a profit.

Stakeholder　A stakeholder is someone with an interest in the future of a business, enterprise, or organization, and usually includes individual customers, borrowers, depositors, investors, employees, shareholders, regulators, and the public.

Standardized Approach   The Standardized Approach to calculate the bank's credit and market risk capital is the simplest approach for calculating these risks that is outlined in the Basel II Accord. For operational risk, "Standardized" refers to an intermediate level approach rather than the simplest approach.

Stress testing   Stress testing assesses the potential outcome of specific changes that are fundamental, material, and adverse.

Swap   A swap is a derivative that enables two counterparties to exchange streams of future cash flows with each other.

Systemically Important Financial Institution (SIFI)   The BIS has defined a list of about 30 banks that are required to add an extra capital buffer under Basel III.

Tier 1 capital   Tier 1 Capital in the Basel Accords is the core capital of the bank and refers to equity capital and to certain types of disclosed reserves as well as particular debt/equity hybrid securities.

Tier 2 capital   Tier 2 Capital in the Basel Accords is supplementary capital and refers to undisclosed and certain disclosed reserves, general provisions, general loan loss reserves, hybrid capital instruments, and subordinated debt.

Tier 3 capital   Tier 3 Capital in the Basel Accords is a specific type of supplementary capital and refers to certain type of short-term debt that can partially satisfy regulatory minimum capital requirements for market risk only. Tier 3 capital was abolished under Basel III.

Trading book   The trading book of a bank is the portfolio of various positions in financial assets, instruments, and commodities that a bank holds with the intention to invest, to trade, or to hedge other positions in the trading book.

Treasury risk   Treasury risk is defined as the risk of loss in the activities of a bank's Treasury.

Treasury   The Treasury manages the financial aspects of an organization and in banking it typically manages the bank's asset and liability structure, liquidity, and capital exposure.

Unencumbered   Free of legal, regulatory, contractual, or other restrictions on the ability of the bank to liquidate, sell, transfer, or assign the asset.

Index